Pelican Books
China Comes of Age

China Comes of Age

JEAN-PIERRE BRULÉ

TRANSLATED BY ROSEMARY SHEED

PENGUIN BOOKS

Penguin Books Ltd, Harmondsworth,
Middlesex, England
Penguin Books Australia Ltd, Ringwood,
Victoria, Australia

La Chine a vingt ans first published by Librairie Arthème Fayard 1969

This translation published 1971

Copyright © Librairie Arthème Fayard, 1969

Translation copyright © Rosemary Sheed, 1971

Made and printed in Great Britain by
Hazell Watson & Viney Ltd, Aylesbury, Bucks
Set in Monotype Ehrhardt

CONTENTS

Foreword 7

1. The Demographic Challenge 11
2. The Economic Challenge 32
3. The Commercial Challenge 65
4. The Military Challenge 92
5. The Nuclear Challenge 128
   Brief Bibliography 165
   Chronology 172

FOREWORD

The first day of October 1949: the proclamation in Peking of the Chinese People's Republic was an event of even wider significance than the October 1917 revolution in Petrograd. The Chinese revolution, which had developed out of the great 'May 4th Movement' of 1919, represents one of the greatest upheavals in the history not just of Asia, but of the whole world.

The various European nations which had spent the past fifty years trying to divide China into zones of influence vanished from the scene once and for all. Ernest Lavisse had warned them: 'All force wears itself out; to be in a position to guide history is no one's permanent right. Europe inherited it from Asia three thousand years ago, but it may not keep it forever.' No one paid any attention to him at the time.

We have lived to see his prophecy come true. Even yesterday's history took place outside Europe – in the U.S.A. and the U.S.S.R.; a new world is now coming to birth in Asia in which Europeans will no longer be masters or leaders.

With Mao Tse-tung's triumph, twenty years ago, the eclipse became total, and a new era began. China since then has been in the centre of world politics; having been forced to accomplish rapid and spectacular economic achievements, unified and renewed by Maoism, not content with being the centre of magnetism for all of Asia (which gazes in admiration at this young giant's achievement), China intends to play its part as a major world power.

After Washington and Moscow, we now have Peking; new

constellations are rising on the horizon of international politics, but we are only half watching. Yet, everything that happens among those three giants must have a more or less immediate repercussion on the quality of life in Europe, since it will ultimately be they who do, or do not, draw us into a universal conflagration.

The dangers we fail to recognize are worse than those we see clearly. If we recognize them, we can take suitable steps to avoid, or at least minimize them, but if we are unaware of them, we are at their mercy.

*

I make no great claims for this book – it is no treatise, no handbook, no first-hand report: it is an attempt briefly to outline the stages of the various transformations China has undergone in the past twenty years, transformations unprecedented in human history.

The usual, and inevitably superficial, features of the travellers' tales our bookshops are flooded with – books written by people who do not speak Chinese and who have visited about six towns – leave room for an essay considering the specific phases of the Chinese challenge on five points: demographic, economic, commercial, military and nuclear; political questions, whether internal or foreign, need enter only in so far as they are closely connected with these, either as a brake or a spur. Since, up until lately, books on China were not considered satisfactory unless they included the suggestion that the Peking regime was on the point of collapse, had little popular support, and was the worst possible government China could have, I have tried in this book, giving facts to support what I say, to put right certain errors that have as a result become fairly widely believed. The only reason for its perhaps not fully expressing my enormous affection for China is my concern to give a 'warts and all' picture.

For that same reason – my concern not to defend any particular 'thesis', but simply to present facts – my prime preoccupation has been with producing evidence. Visual experiences, interviews with many different kinds of people, direct contacts with individuals in the countryside and in the factories – I have drawn on all these. For written sources, I have studied the major works on Communist China published in the U.S.A., the U.S.S.R. and, above all, in Japan. Furthermore, I have given as much space as possible to the local Chinese press, an indispensable source of information and the most vivid of all.

The strict discipline of History as learnt at the Sorbonne from men who were my friends as well as my instructors, and who have been an inestimable influence upon me – an influence that will certainly be felt in this book – will, I trust, enable me to measure up to some extent to the task I have set myself.

In conclusion, I must express my thanks to all those who have helped me in so many ways, in Peking, in Moscow, in Tokyo and in Washington.

ONE. THE DEMOGRAPHIC CHALLENGE

It is a good thing for China to have a large population. Even if our population becomes several times its present size, China is well able to find a solution, and that solution is production. Of all the valuable things in the world, people are the most valuable of all . . .

Mao Tse-tung

While the very existence of China has made itself more felt in the world than ever before, the fact of the demographic pressure inside China has become an imponderable more disturbing than ever for the future, indeed a problem whose solution must be of concern to everyone. Already, one human being in four is Chinese. In China itself, humanity is present everywhere; a slow silting up, if one can so describe it, of population has, over the course of centuries, gone into the formation of this vast mass of Chinese.

Demographic Acceleration

Twenty-three centuries before our era, there were some thirteen and a half million Chinese; it is estimated that in the first century A.D. there were 50 million, and this estimated figure was to remain fairly steady from the Han dynasty (202 B.C.–A.D. 220) up to the Ming (1368–1644). With the advent of the Manchu dynasty in 1644, the first census revealed 143 million inhabitants. And from then on, the quantitative factor was to be of enormous importance: 300 million Chinese in 1787, 430 million in 1850 and, at the fall of the empire in 1911, 374 million.

Population-counting in China is no novelty; indeed, ever since 1644 there has existed a register for doing so. Families were grouped in tens, with ten tens forming a hundred, ten hundreds a thousand, and each thousand having as its head an elected member whose duty it was to keep a check on the numbers of people in the group, and also what work was being done. This man would record any changes (deaths, births, marriages, arrivals and departures) and pass them on to a higher authority, who would in turn pass them on to the Central Government. This, the *Bao tsia* system, was in force for two centuries, and it was by that means that it was known that the population of China, first estimated as 143 million, had reached 430 million by 1850. After that date, information became harder to come by, and less reliable: governors would tend to overestimate the population of their provinces, to increase their own importance.

By a decree of 27 May 1928, the Nanking Government endeavoured to make a complete census, organized by the police – but such were the conditions under which it was done, that the results are quite useless. Certainly, local customs did nothing to make things easier; for instance, it was common for daughters from poor families to be established from adolescence onwards in the homes of the better-off as maids, and they had no names of their own but were simply known as 'X's wife', or 'X's mother'. Then too, there was another custom whereby a newborn child was considered as a year old on the day of his birth; but since, on the other hand, one's age was reckoned not by the day one was born, but by the first day of the year, a child born on New Year's eve would have his 'second birthday' the next day. And in some areas, the statistics would be changed by the omission of all children under a year old, or perhaps of all girls under five, and so on. In such conditions it was physically impossible to get valid figures, so the authorities had to be content with estimating: 466 million people in 1934, and 479 million in 1936.

When the People's Republic came into being, on 1 October 1949, and more and more people were enrolled in the Communist Party, it seemed that conditions at last existed for a scientifically based census. Furthermore, the Central Committee of the Communist Party needed statistics in order to set its economic plans on foot, and to prepare for the 1954 general elections. So, the Chinese Central Bureau of Statistics copied the methods used by the Soviets in their 1939 census: in fact it was a Soviet statistics expert, S. K. Krotevitch, who helped the Chinese officials carrying out the census to do their job –

there were two and a half million of them, apart from party volunteers. It was finalized on the night of 30 June–1 July 1953, and was far more precise than anything had ever been before; so much so, indeed, that Professor Alfred Sauvy, of the Collège de France, and Director of the National Institute for Demographic Studies, declared: 'Even in the West, no census has been conducted with such absolute precision.' It certainly filled an important gap, given that a quarter of the world's population lives in China.

The Census of 30 June 1953

The results of the census were beyond anyone's wildest predictions: at midnight on 30 June, the world contained 601,938,035 Chinese, 582,604,000 of them in the People's Republic, plus 11,740,000 living elsewhere, and 7,591,000 Formosans. Peking's 582 million included national minorities – 6 per cent of the whole, i.e., 35,320,000. The world suddenly realized the vastness of China, with a population three times the size of Russia, and four times that of the U.S.A.

Various interesting points emerge from the 1953 census. For instance, with 302 million men and 280 million women, the proportion of women is notably lower than that of men – 48 per cent as against 52 per cent. This disproportion is the result, still persisting today, of the age-old inferiority of women; mortality was always very much higher in girls than in boys up to the advent of the Maoist regime, which enforces absolute equality between the sexes.

The population of China is extremely young; two out of five are under 18; and the proportion of over-sixties is something like 7 or 8 per cent of the total. The same would be true in India or Egypt, whereas in France and Sweden, the proportion of old people is two or three times larger (17 per cent now, and soon 20 per cent more). The classic pyramid of the ages, with enormous numbers in the youngest groups, to be seen in China is that of a country at its fullest demographic vitality. Comparison with France (see graph on p. 17) makes this even clearer: the people of working age (15–55 years) in China represent

52–3 per cent of the population (as against 50 per cent in 1930).

With an urban population of only 13·26 per cent, China may look like one of the least urbanized states in the world. Yet, with 77 million people living in conurbations, it still has the third largest urban population in the world (after the U.S.A. and the U.S.S.R.). The population density of something like 80 people per square kilometre is large for so rural a country, but it is a deceptive figure, for the population is not uniformly spread out over the whole land area of the country. Thus, we find

Population of China by Sex and Age at 30 June 1953*

(Figures are in millions)

Age groups	Males	Females	Total
0–4 years	46·8	44·1	90·9
5–9 years	33·8	30	63·7
10–14 years	29·6	25·2	54·7
15–19 years	28	25	53
20–24 years	25	23·1	48·1
25–29 years	24	21·1	45·1
30–34 years	21·4	18·8	40·1
35–39 years	19·4	17·9	37·3
40–44 years	16·7	15·6	32·3
45–49 years	14·9	14·3	29·3
50–54 years	12·7	12·1	24·8
55–59 years	10·6	10·3	20·9
60–64 years	8·2	8·7	16·9
65–69 years	5·5	6·4	11·9
70–74 years	3·4	4·6	8
75–79 years	1·5	2·2	3·7
80–84 years	0·5	0·8	1·2
85 years and over	0·2	0·4	0·6
All ages	302·1	280·5	582·6

* The figures given are estimated to the nearest round number; thus the sum of the figures for males and females does not, in some cases, correspond to the totals.

*Population Distribution in the Regions**

Administrative area	Capital	Area in sq. km.	Population in thousands
Anhwei	Hofei	139,900	33·560
Shansi	Yangku (Talyuan)	157,100	15·960
Shantung	Tsinan	153,300	54·030
Shensi	Sian	195,800	18·100
Fukien	Foochow (Minhow)	123,100	14·650
Heilungkiang	Harbin (Pinkiang)	463,600	14·860
Honan	Chengchow	167,000	48·670
Hopeh	Peking	212,800	44·720
Hunan	Changsha	210,500	36·220
Hupeh	Wuhan	187,500	30·790
Kansu	Lanchow	432,900	12·800
Kiangsi	Nanchang	164,800	18·610
Kiangsu	Nanking	107,300	45·230
Kirin	Kirin (Yungki)	187,000	12·550
Kwangtung	Canton	231,400	37·960
Kweichow	Kweiyang	174,000	16·890
Liaoning	Shenyang (Mukden)	207,000	24·090
Szechwan	Chengtu	834,000	72·160
Chekiang	Hangchow	101,800	25·280
Tsinghai (Chinghai)	Hsining	721,000	2·050
Yunnan	Kunming	436,000	19·100
Kwangsi (autonomous region)	Nanning (Yungning)	220,400	19·390
Inner Mongolia (autonomous region)	Huhehot (Kweisui)	1,834,500	9·200
Ninghsia (autonomous region)	Yinchuan (Ninghsia)	66,800	1·810
Sinkiang (autonomous region)	Urumchi	1,646,800	5·640
Tibet (autonomous region)	Lhasa	1,485,600	1·270
Peking		8,770	4·010
Shanghai		700	6·900

*Administratively people's China today is divided into 22 provinces (one of them being Taiwan, i.e., Formosa, having 12 million people in an area of 36,000 square kilometres), plus 5 autonomous regions, and two special municipalities (which have the status of provinces): Peking and Shanghai.

densities of 200 people per square kilometre in the great northern plain; some areas achieve the fantastic figure of 1,000 per square kilometre (round the mouth of the Yang-tse) and even up to 1,200 in some cantons of Kwangtung (which has the highest rural density in the world). As we move west, we find the density decreases, and in Tibet, for instance, there are only 1 or 2 people per square kilometre. The break-up of the figures into administrative units shows how one province can vary from another (see table on p. 15). A glance at the map shows that the largest densities are in the cultivated lands of the south – one of the major features of China's human geography – due to the twofold influence of rice-growing and the climate. Such a demographic explosion must present innumerable problems to a developing country: can the standard of living be raised (which obviously demands an enormous increase in the national income) faster than the population is increasing? That is *the* problem above all others.

Control: Yes or No?

Both Chinese and foreign estimates reckon the present rate of population increase as being 2 per cent per year, which means at present a yearly addition of 12 to 15 million people. At this rate, there will be a thousand million people in China in 1981. According to the U.N. estimates, the Chinese population was 700 million in 1961, and Dr S. Chandrasekhar, the eminent Indian demographer, accepts that figure; here is his estimate:

1956: 630 million	1966: 770 million	1976: 930 million
1961: 700 million	1971: 850 million	1981: 1,000 million

The population figures given in the above table are those announced when the administrative division was made at the end of 1958, as reported by Jen Yu-ti in *The Geography of China* (Foreign Language Publications, Peking, 1965).

I have let them stand, for it would be unwise to assume that every province had been subjected to the natural average growth rate (2·3 per cent per year) of the population as a whole. Given our ignorance of movement inside the country (which is not, as it was in the past, connected with natural disasters, but planned to provide a better distribution of manpower) all such figures must be treated with the utmost caution.

Pyramid of Ages in China and France

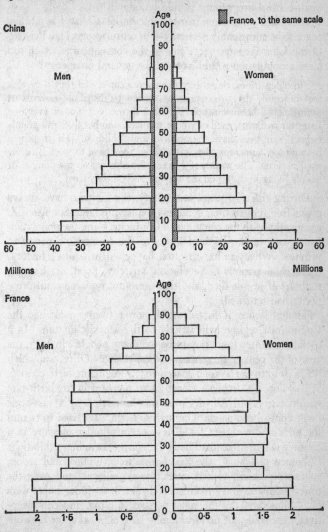

The leaders in Peking have to face the question of whether China can let its population continue to grow, or whether a birth-control programme should be established.

We know that from time immemorial China has always practised Malthusianism: twenty-four centuries ago, Han Fei-tsu, of the Chu dynasty, wrote this of the consequences which too large a population would have on the general prosperity:

... in olden times, there were not many people, and they were rich and peaceful; the government never had to distribute rewards or punishments, because people governed themselves. Today, everyone longs for five sons, each of whom will have another five, and grandfathers will thus have twenty-five grandchildren. But if people become too numerous, they grow poor; they have to work hard for small returns. The wealth of a nation depends not on the number of people living in it, but on the amount of food they have ...

During times of peace and plenty, the Chinese have always given free rein to their fondness for having large families – in conformity with the teachings of Confucius – and the population has grown to the furthest limits of the country's capacity to produce. When, as has so often happened in China's history, there were periods of revolution, anarchy, flood, or drought, millions of people died, and they were not replaced until prosperity had returned.

Though when it first came to power twenty years ago the Communist regime held strictly to the Marxist dictum: 'In a socialist country there cannot be too many people', in 1953, the year of the census, there was a radical change of direction which was to lead to the law of 7 March 1957 recognizing birth control. It was hoped to achieve a drop of 50 per cent in the birth-rate within ten years! All of China was inundated by a vast-scale birth-control campaign. The marriage-age was raised to twenty for boys and eighteen for girls – not a popular measure in a country where fifteen had been the norm. Travelling exhibitions ('Women of China', the Red Cross, trade unions, and so on, sponsoring them) visited cities, towns, villages, and even the tiniest hamlets, to try to create a change in attitude. There were talks, illustrated by the most persuasive films, and contraceptives were sold, but no *ideal* family size, no *ideal* space between children was ever proposed to future parents. The stress was laid mainly on welfare (too many children makes it hard for a woman to work, and damages the well-being of the family). It may seem odd that a system which puts the interests of the people above those of the individual should have realized that only considerations of individual welfare would be compelling – but China is a country where nothing should surprise one. However, the sexual habits of a people cannot be changed overnight – as we also see in the countries of the Third World – and in China this was particularly difficult because all its past traditions had favoured large families.

Quite soon, in fact, the campaign came to an end, and in 1958, the Government returned to Marxist orthodoxy. The *Red Flag*, the doctrinal organ of the Communist Party, explained the reversal of policy thus: 'President Mao realized long ago that, in a country that is underdeveloped economically, a large population is a help rather than a hindrance to increasing development.' (*Hongqi*, No. 9, 1958). So China was back to the populationist doctrine with arguments that seem to have been taken from Jean Bodin: 'The only real power and wealth is human beings.' The Dean of Peking University, Professor Ma Ying-chu, who a year earlier, in his *A New Principle of Population*, had used arguments based on the lack of capital accumulation in people's China, and the probabilities of vast-scale industrial unemployment in the future, suddenly found himself castigated as 'reactionary and defeatist'; Mao declared that the Chinese had not only 'one mouth, but two arms'. As earlier in Russia, the official Chinese press maintained an almost total silence on the topic. The ten-yearly census could not be held in 1963 – because of the economic recession still remaining from the 'black' years, 1959–61 – but took place in 1964, without any results being made public. People looked back longingly to 1953 when the census, though perhaps not perfect, had at least the merit of being available. Now, they had to try to get approximations by looking at the population development in different ways, for while the death rate could be assessed more or less correctly, the birth rate was not so easy. According to Mrs Li Teh-chuan, Minister of Health, the population of China increases by 15 million a year. With an estimated birth rate of 3·7 per cent, and a decreasing mortality rate, the increase would therefore be more than 2 per cent per year – which would have been an astonishingly high figure before 1939, but which is surpassed by a number of countries today (Brazil, Mexico, Turkey, Formosa, the Philippines, etc.). If we accept this rate, that is, an increase of about 15 million per year, it is possible to estimate with some certainty that the Chinese population will have been 756 million in 1965 and 820 million in 1969. We may recall that the Chinese Prime Minister, Chou En-lai, declared to an Indonesian leader, Ali Sastroamidjojo, on 27 April 1965: 'Indonesia, North Korea, North Vietnam and East Germany, together with China, form a bloc of 900 million people.' Now the total population of the other countries he named amounted to 150 million, so both logic and arithmetic lead us to deduce 750 million for China. Thus the head of Government himself was indirectly confirming the figure of 15 million per year which had been given a few years earlier by his Minister of Health.

So the Chinese leaders, aware of the vast and complex problems with which overpopulation would soon face them, discreetly but firmly returned to their birth-control propaganda. The Government even resorted to a step which really follows a suggestion from Confucius, six centuries before Christ: that of still further retarding the age of marriage fixed for boys at twenty and girls at eighteen. Dr Yeh Kung-Chao, Professor in the Medical College of Peking, expressed the official point of view in the paper *Chinese Youth* – with the economic motive carefully disguised by social and health arguments:

... I suggest that women should, in general, have their first child at the age of twenty-six or twenty-seven, and then a second three or five years later. If they live in very comfortable circumstances, they might have a third child in another three to five years. They will then be perhaps thirty-four or thirty-five. ... As for the question of how many children one ought to have, I think that, taking the mother's health and the upbringing of the child as our prime concerns, generally the answer should be no more than two. We should have fewer children, but more beautiful ones. If conditions are right, one could consider having a third child, but it is better not to have more than three. ... Thus, generally speaking, there is much to be said for marrying later and practising birth control. In the short term, this preserves the health of parents and children, and makes for happier family life; in the longer term, it makes it possible for young people to give themselves fully to building up socialism, and creating favourable conditions for the growth and education of the coming generation ...

(*Chungkuo Chingnien Bao*, 21 July 1962)

So, Chinese men and women are now being 'invited' not to marry before the ages of thirty and twenty-five respectively. In demographic terms, if the Government limits the child-bearing period of the Chinese couple, there will follow smaller families. An effective method indeed of controlling the population growth! However, the Chinese peasant is not too delighted by such measures: they deprive him of his security in old age, and the joy of seeing a large family about him.

Also it must not be forgotten that, at the stage at which the Chinese are now, the population must either grow rapidly, or become heavily weighted with older people; if it does not want to age (if, that is, it wants to preserve a balance between young and old), then it will have to double every twenty years (which would mean that in a hundred years there would be 100,000 million Chinese). To double so large a population every twenty years would certainly present problems. In their concern for the future, the Chinese, who already present a problem to the world by their size and their power, will become a really heavy burden in the years to come. It is therefore extremely important that we watch most carefully the demographic phenomenon of China, and the battle between populationists and birth-controllers now raging there.

The Emancipation of the Chinese Woman

The demographic policy of the Peking Government is thus aiming at two objectives: the need to make use of a vast mass of labour (to guard against economic weakness) and the need to maintain a reasonable balance between the number of consumers and the amount of food produced. The 1962 campaign against early marriages is a perfect illustration of this; the stress laid on making the utmost use of women workers made available by female emancipation is another reminder of the same preoccupation.

One must not forget that the coming to power of the Communists in October 1949, and the law on marriage seven months later, were greeted as a real liberation by Chinese women. To appreciate this fully, one must recall some of the terrifying ways in which women were really treated as no more than animals in China in the past. The poet, Fu Hsuan rightly wrote: 'How sad it is to be born a woman! Nothing on earth is of less value . . .' In the tenth century A.D. the curious practice of foot-binding was introduced into China, to stop women's feet from growing. One need only look at those who have been subjected to it recently to realize that, though the direct object of it was not to make women too weak to emerge from their homes, such was in fact the result. With the slogan: 'Set free your feet', the Communist Party – needing the female labour-force – fought against footbinding, and abolished it in every area they controlled.

In China in the past, the birth of a girl was thought of as a curse. And since a girl baby was a burden, a nuisance, a useless object, she would be drowned or in some other manner done away with. Even when girls were not killed, they would be less well looked after than boys, hence the astonishingly high mortality rate among women, whose consequences can still be observed today (see Table on p. 14).

Marriages were arranged in early childhood, and since the future couple were not consulted at all, marriage became a matter between two families – a business matter, in fact, since the advantages to be gained were obviously the prime concern. It was a kind of sale, not unlike a sale of livestock: presents (silver, produce of some kind, cloth, jewellery, and so on) costing a lot to the boy's family, would be looked upon mainly as a deposit to secure the marriage; as soon as the wedding had actually taken place, the boy's mother expected her daughter-in-law to work hard so as to repay the money spent on bringing her into the family. A girl would therefore be betrothed extremely early – because she was cheaper then – and the boy's family, treating her as a servant, would be amply repaid, in fact, more than repaid, for what they had spent on her. Marriage, far from ensuring the equality of the partners, made a woman completely subject to her husband. The couple could not, for instance, hang their clothes on the same peg; while they might eat the same food, it must not be from the same dishes. Even sexual relations were very strictly regulated: the husband had to perform his conjugal duty following a set protocol worked out in detail by the ritualists; it would be his generosity that dictated the frequency of their intercourse. And it would be an appalling scandal for a husband and wife to have a bath together . . .

These are only a few of the innumerable examples which help to show why Chinese women saw the coming of Mao, and the abolition of this feudal system of marriage, as a real emancipation. Furthermore, the reforms intended to alter women's conditions, to make them the equals of their menfolk in every sphere, when in the past they had been inferior – no more than slaves to procreation, merchandise to be sold – were their own best recommendation for achieving success. Mao, faithful to Lenin's teaching, was well aware of this, and in the Constitution of 7 November 1931 for the Chinese Soviet Republic of Kiangsi, he inserted an article proclaiming the emancipation of women, and making various rules that would help them to take their full part in social, economic and political life. The Chinese Communist leaders were faithful to their promises, and the law on marriage (eight chapters, with twenty-seven articles in all) was promulgated on 1 May 1950 by the Peking Government. Since the new regime had freed them from the slavery of the past thousand years or more, the women of China gave it their total support. But this new law, stopping the marriage of children, giving equal rights in the home to both partners, allowing each party freedom to choose the other, forbidding that any wife be ill-treated either by her husband or her mother-in-law, in short totally over-throwing the structures and customs of centuries, still met with a lot of opposition. The law on marriage, the first major measure taken by the country's new rulers, was to take far more time and patience to put fully into effect than it took to compose. A great many girls who tried to exercise the rights given them by law were murdered; others were driven to suicide by enraged husbands, or by elderly parents disturbed by this abandonment of male supremacy; many young people of both sexes killed themselves because their families refused to let them marry the person they wished. A report by Chou En-lai, on 25 February 1953, mentions that between 70 and 80 thousand people committed suicide in 1952 alone because of family or marriage problems! But in a country as vast as China such cases can only have appeared as isolated instances.

The marriage law, in establishing a wholly new society, did away once and for all with the ancestral Chinese clan pattern, changing it to a more Western form, with this important difference that the family was larger than its own narrow framework, and part of a nuclear cell for production and revolution. Article 8 is especially significant.* By ordering that the couple work together to build a new society, it makes clear that individuals are totally dedicated parts of a collective movement, and it assumes all kinds of duties and obligations attaching to individuals thus harnessed for the work of the community. The primacy of political and economic structures is quite clear: the need to increase production makes it necessary for the individual to subordinate exclusively family interests to those of the welfare of society as a whole. The reform of marriage which was borne along on the whirlwind of the reform of land-ownership, the second stone in the Communist structure, was to make women full citizens: more than 150 million Chinese women are working in the people's communes. Henceforth, in matters of civic rights, family, production, work, salary, security (welfare services, etc.), women were to be in every way equal to men. This advancement for women can be best seen perhaps from a few statistics: the Eighth Party Congress in 1956 counted 3 million women labourers and white-collar workers, 764,000 women cadres, and 70,000 officials and intellectuals. (The party at that time had 10,720,000 members.) Eleven thousand women were

---

* Article 8: 'The partners have a duty to love and respect one another, help and support one another through life, live in harmony, share in the work of production, bring up their children and all work together for the welfare of the family and the building of a new society.'

employed in higher education: 40 per cent in the faculties of medicine and pharmacy, and 18 per cent in those of the sciences and in the polytechnics. Secondary and primary teaching employed respectively 33,000 and 348,000 women. In the legal world, there were 144 women presidents of the courts, and another 1,700 ordinary judges. The medical services occupied some 850,000 women. Among the 340,000 women in the civil service, 40,000 were high-ranking officials. Since they could now both vote and be elected, women took an active part in political life: 90 per cent voted in the 1964 election, and the National Assembly that election put into office included 542 female deputies (17·8 per cent of the total as compared with 12·2 per cent in the previous election). The Vice-President of the Republic is a woman, Mrs Sung Ching-ling; a number of women are deputy ministers in the Peking Central Government, while another 300 are members of local governments. The Cultural Revolution brought two women to the very front rank of the political scene – Chiang Ching and Yeh Chun (in private life Mrs Mao and Mrs Lin Piao) – making them among the fourteen people who actually wield supreme power, the former being No. 6, the latter No. 12, according to the list of precedence published on 1 April 1969 for the Ninth Party Congress. Teng Yin-chao (Mrs Chou En-lai), who was a notable speaker and very active in the fifties, is for the moment keeping in the background.

Clearly women now play a very active part in the political sphere. The moment there is any danger of heresy or conservatism, women come on the scene: novels and films indicate the preponderant role played by women in the formation of the new society. Even the little girls in the Young Pioneer movement, proudly wearing their red sashes, police the public gardens, and the firmness with which they remove the crowds of excited children who gather round white strangers in the square in Peking has to be seen to be believed!

Chinese women, free of the constraints of the past, allowed to emerge from their houses and farms, are becoming educated. Adult courses are proliferating, and so are dispensaries and maternity hospitals. And the next generation will be abundantly supplied with crèches, primary schools, secondary and higher education. However, though freed from their former rulers – fathers, husbands or mothers-in-law – Chinese women now have another strict and rigid boss: the State. Work is hard and exhausting, and will continue so until it is lightened by mechanization. So, though one hardly ever finds parents interfering in marriages nowadays, one finds instead the Communist Party doing so in its gradual raising of the marriage age. Production is the prime need, and must certainly come before reproduction! As long as the economy is weak, despite the fact that millions of women previously confined to domestic work are now manning farms and factories (and one must not forget that the regime has only been going for twenty years), full emancipation for women must remain a promise for the future. But though today's women may not reap the reward of their struggles and sufferings, at least they can feel that their daughters and granddaughters will do so. And that is reward enough.

The Chinese Abroad

The large colonies of Chinese settled abroad, especially in south-east Asia, pose a major problem. The emigration movement began in the fifteenth century with the development of trade routes, and in the 1953 census the total number who left is reckoned at 11,743,000. Today there are some 20 million Chinese – as many as the entire population of Canada – living outside China, 18 million of them in south-east Asia, where the demographic imbalance is already alarming. This diaspora – more enforced than freely chosen – spread over sixty-two countries in five continents, includes a good number of firmly established communities with traditions of their own. These Chinese communities 'across the sea' (*Hua Chiao*) have existed from time immemorial.

Even before the discovery of America, Chinese from what are now the southern provinces of Fukien and Kwangtung, had flocked to the new promised land of Nan Yang, or as we call it, south-east Asia. Such a flood, in some ways comparable with the Jewish Diaspora, was not always well liked by the Chinese

Government: the emigrants often found themselves considered as *chien min*, traitors, by the Chinese authorities. By the time the Europeans got there, the Chinese were firmly established all over south-east Asia. The economic development which accompanied the presence of Westerners, in combination with the work of a Chinese labour-force (in exploiting raw materials and the natural wealth of the land), was to do a lot to improve their conditions. And gradually almost all the small businesses, and the major part of international commerce, came into the hands of the efficient and hard-working Chinese, there to remain. These expatriate Chinese, generally well established in the host country, but not assimilated, though they only represent something like 5 or 6 per cent of the total population, are so economically powerful as to have an influence quite out of proportion to their numbers.

It seems to me that we have not sufficiently recognized the strange parallelism between this southern-Chinese emigration, and the European colonization of the same south-east Asian countries. By bringing their money and their technology, the Europeans created a demand for labour in plantations, in mines and in business; so the Chinese emigration was, in the last quarter of the nineteenth century, to reach a scale previously unheard of. But it also changed in nature, by developing into closed groups; instead of marrying local women and merging into the local population, the Chinese began bringing out Chinese women, and founding Chinese families. Though extremely diversified, these Chinese communities abroad are among the best-organized groups in the world. They have their own family, regional and provincial associations, their own welfare organizations; and, in countries with large Chinese colonies, their own chambers of commerce, forming a kind of state within a state; they also have their own schools, corporations, guilds, employers' associations, trade unions, friendly societies and even secret societies. Though there are diversities within the community, they will still always present a common front to the native population. Though three quarters of them were born in the countries they live in, and are therefore not immigrants, they remain like immigrants, clinging to their language and their customs, and above all, especially since red China has become a major power, to their loyalty to their fatherland; in other words they cannot ever be assimilated because they are determined to *be* Chinese. Hence the defence-mechanisms they arouse in the host countries.

The problem is that, in states only recently made independent – whether non-aligned (Burma, Cambodia, India, Indonesia, Laos), satellite (Pakistan, the Philippines), or somewhere between (Malaysia) – power is now in the hands of native nationalist groups who obviously have no intention of allowing the Chinese to continue to dominate the economic life of their countries, and want to assimilate all foreign minorities as fast as possible. Typical of this is Indonesia, where General Sukharto has forced the Chinese immigrants to take Javanese-sounding names. There can be no doubt that the Chinese abroad are now expected to play a major part in all the decisions concerning the future of the countries where they now live. They are now vulnerable minorities, but might they become a tool in Maoist strategy, providing Peking with a fifth column in other countries?

The development of Chinese nationalism since the beginning of this century has certainly influenced the Chinese in other countries tremendously, and thus strengthened the ties that link them with home. Sun Yat-sen's revolutionary movement, and later on the Nationalist Government, received huge sums of money from them, and representatives from Chinese communities abroad were also deputies in the Chinese parliament, by the principle of *jus sanguinis* adopted by the first Chinese code of nationality. When the Communists came to power, twenty years ago, their attitude to the Chinese abroad changed; obviously they still watch them closely, but whereas in 1954, Peking's attitude to them was almost one of threat, since then it has become different. The 1953 census having included them in the Chinese population, they have deputies in the Peking National Assembly. The 1954 constitution, in Article 98, states: 'The People's Republic of China protects the rights and interests of citizens living abroad.' This poses problems both for the emigrants themselves, and for their hosts. At home there is a huge organization concerned with the emigrants, the Overseas

Chinese Affairs Commission, whose president (at present Liao Cheng-cheh, who was elected on 4 January 1965) has the rank and privileges of a minister. This organization is particularly concerned in the establishment of villages (state farms) for Chinese coming home; it deals with the children of emigrants who want to have a Chinese education, and also watches over the business interests and investments and any money sent home by the emigrants. Attached to this Commission are three special organizations from the Central Committee of the Communist Party, and a number of friendly societies, especially in the large towns in the south. In the international sphere, especially in countries where relations are not specially 'friendly', red China will respond actively and at times violently to any decision that goes counter to the interests of its emigrants.

By acting thus, Peking preserves its reputation as the great protector of Chinese rights abroad and its responses will vary with the situation: vigorous, where vigour will be of some use, and turning a blind eye (as in Malaysia for instance) when that suits Maoist policy better. In its great strategy for world revolution, China has discovered a most valuable tool in its emigrants. Being so numerous and so well established, they form a major factor in Peking's twofold battle: political (in the policies of south-east Asia) and economic (in the money they send home, a vital element for the Chinese balance of payments). Though the sums sent home which, before the Second World War, reached some 100 million dollars, are not so large today, they still represent a goodly total: every community is bound to pay a given sum in tax to the Chinese Bank in Hong Kong. There is certainly no force used, yet every emigrant who wants to be buried in the land of his ancestors willingly pays the tax. However, the fact that the Chinese abroad are willing thus to raise funds for the home country does not necessarily mean that they give it their political allegiance.

Though the Chinese abroad – the majority of them, at least – are at present careful to avoid any political commitment, the possibility of an eventual conquest by China of all or part of Asia, or more simply, the generalized fear inspired by Peking, means that Chinese immigrants are considered as potential vipers in the bosom. Everywhere – often quite unjustly – they are under suspicion, with at times catastrophic consequences – as for instance in September–October 1965, the Indonesian massacres in which the Chinese immigrants, together with all members or sympathizers or even supposed sympathizers of the Indonesian Communist Party, fell victim to the same blood bath. The nationalist leaders of the new states have to direct their energies against a single enemy in order to maintain their national unity – it used to be colonialism and is now Maoism – and they identify their position on the chessboard of Asia more and more in relation to their nearest powerful neighbour (the distance factor plays an important part in foreign policy); consequently, they are forcing the Chinese immigrants to consider themselves as merely tolerated for their business acumen and their importance in finance and industry, and the immigrants will inevitably tend to seek support from home, and thus to show more national loyalty than in the past. In a word, the Chinese immigrants' guide is opportunism: many are prepared to swear fidelity to the host country if circumstances favour their doing so, but are equally prepared to turn to Peking if not. They may well take part in local activities, join trade unions – depending on their connections – or even work with the Communists of the country; thus, for months or even years to come, the political attitude of the Chinese abroad will remain a key factor in the development of south-east Asia. A solution to the problem could yet, with care, be achieved without too many difficulties or frictions; but if mishandled, it could well be (to borrow one of Mao's 'thoughts') 'that spark that can set fire to a whole prairie'. For, though at present Peking is too weak to intervene effectively, it will be a different matter when China has an army, navy and air force equipped for attack as well as for defence.

The Power of Numbers

But the question remains: can those thousand million Chinese who will exist in the next ten years be kept within their own present borders?

Under the Han dynasty (202 B.C.–A.D. 220) China was more or less the size it is now. Yet there have never been any 'great invasions' by the Chinese: before yielding to the temptation to conquer foreign land, China still has land of its own to colonize. Up to now, China has colonized its own provinces. Remember how in Manchuria (reunited with China in 1644 with the advent of the Manchu dynasty) there was a flood of a million Chinese a year between 1910 and 1931. For the first time in its history, the railway enabled the country to embark on the totally new adventure – since in the past all migration had always been southwards – of colonizing the north. Today, in Manchuria (its borders fixed in January 1956, it is also called North-east China, and contains the three provinces of Heilungkiang, Kirin, and Liaoning) there are still only 3 million Manchurians out of a population of 60 million! The Kremlin is intensely conscious of this example of Chinese colonization; it is so close to the vast area of Siberia with its immense and barely tapped resources. So Moscow guards its eastern frontier (some 10,000 kilometres), by strengthening military units, building air bases and rocket launching pads, and also by a massive programme of Russification, settling enormous numbers of Russians and Ukrainians in the area. There is certainly no question of Moscow offering its wide-open spaces to China. Yet already, a contemporary writer, Chen Pi-cheng, has suggested a further move south, finding the Burmese 'triangle' very attractive, and even beyond the countries where Chinese have gone before where there is land ready and waiting: Borneo (with 746 square kilometres and 2 million people), New Guinea (785,000 square kilometres and 2 million people), and then there is Australia – to say nothing of the rich lands of Madagascar and Africa ...

There is one peaceful solution possible: to fill the world with Chinese as it was once filled by the English, the French, the Portuguese, in the days of empire-building – which would give Peking a power over the world that would have been unimaginable before. It is easy enough to see the importance of the Chinese demographic challenge: on it may well depend the fate of the entire world.

TWO. THE ECONOMIC CHALLENGE

It is an arduous task to provide an adequate standard of living for hundreds of millions of Chinese, and to transform our country which is behindhand economically into a prosperous one.

Mao Tse-tung

Twenty years: that seems long enough for us to try to make an approximate assessment of the transformations – unprecedented in history – that have combined to overthrow all the social and economic structures of the former Middle Empire. Following the marriage law, the next cardinal point of the revolution was agrarian reform. It was thought that if only the peasants could bring about the development of the largest underdeveloped country in the world – a country with provinces as different as Denmark is from Spain, and whose natural situation is not a favourable one – then the People's Republic could prove its ability to do something totally new; the important thing was to beware of all preconceived ideas, however much they might have been proved valid in Russia.

Any belief in the need for uniformity in agricultural conditions and development in a Communist regime must be dismissed, for the regime must, while setting a world record for vast-scale agricultural improvement, also create an industry proportionate to the size of the country. Thus, people's China is the only Communist country in which agriculture and industry are being developed simultaneously, as expressed in the slogan: 'We must walk on two feet.' In the following paragraphs I shall be considering the amazing changes in agriculture and industry, and I shall do so at some length, because our normal channels of information have tended to over-simplify them to a misleading extent. I, on the other hand, want especially to stress certain characteristics that are peculiar to the economic evolution of people's China, because they throw more light on the radical transformations that have taken place than any series of textbooks or discussions of economic theory.

Statistics, of course, are indispensable to any economic analysis. The only official Chinese economic statistics are collected in *The Ten Great Years*, published in 1960, and covering the period 1949–58 – the first ten years of the regime. The definite figures from the Central Office of Statistics can be taken as wholly reliable for industry, but less so for agriculture, since the system whereby statistical information is gleaned in the country areas has never worked very well. In 1958, the Government had handed over the responsibility for the provision of statistics to the local party committees, and since then no definite figures have been published. One must therefore work as best one can with the percentages of increase – official, but partial – given in ministerial speeches or the local press.

Figures from Soviet or Anglo-Saxon sources are virtually useless, so I have turned to Japanese sources for the second ten years of the regime. Japan, having contributed largely to modern Chinese industry – in Manchuria, for instance – understands its origins and structures. Furthermore, as the first business partner of people's China, Japan has been obliged to make an objective study of the Chinese economy. And, finally, since there are numerous Japanese business agents in China, their country is the only one in a position to get hold of reliable economic information. Thus, despite the many obstacles, I have been able to assemble enough evidence to attempt to give a general survey of the Chinese economy over the past twenty years.

A. AGRARIAN REFORM: THE REAL HINGE OF THE REVOLUTION

Our agrarian revolution has followed and will continue to follow this process: the land-owning class who possess the land are changed into a landless class, and the landless peasants become small land-owners by being given the confiscated land ... The private property of the peasants, in turn, will be transformed into community property with socialist agriculture: this has already happened in the Soviet Union, and will finally take place all over the world.

Mao Tse-tung

Simply by the weight of its population, China is bound to influence the fate of every one of us, for if its demographic growth continues as it is, and its agriculture lags behind, the results will be incalculable. If, on the other hand, its agricultural development is such as to satisfy the needs of its swarming humanity, people's China will provide a compelling example for the starving peoples of Africa and Asia. (In the world today, a child dies of hunger every 42 seconds; 16 per cent of the world's inhabitants consume 70 per cent of its wealth, while the remaining 84 per cent have to make do with the other 30 per cent.) It is vital, therefore, that we waste no time in assessing the measure of the Chinese agricultural challenge.

Farmers for Four Thousand Years

'The peasant – civilization's pack-horse': that was how Trotsky put it. Chinese annalists honour agriculture as the basis of all the professions, and recognize the farmer as *the* essential worker, second in the social hierarchy of scholars, farmers, merchants, artisans – a quadri-partite structure that has existed now for forty years. Agriculture in China thus has a treasury of experience to call on, the accumulation of generations of patient and wise peasants. That is why, having produced more than five thousand harvests, the fields of China are still workable. Many civilizations have vanished without managing to erode them. It is certainly no common success in the history of the world's agriculture to have kept land fertile for four thousand years.

Everything in China bears witness to the closeness of man to nature. And ultimately it is man – and not the soil, the vegetation, or the climate – who constitutes the most characteristic element in the Chinese countryside. But though, today, China is literally swarming with peasant workers, there has been a radical change since the Communist regime took over in the empirical methods followed by their ancestors. Such radical change was needed if China was to adopt the innovations that must be made, and preserve only that from the past which might be useful in the present. When China came wholly under the rule of the

Peking Government, its outstanding feature was still the poverty of the peasants. In a country comprising 960 million hectares,* only 100 million of which were cultivated by some 500 million people (the average holding being 1·5 hectares, as against 16 in Denmark), the agrarian problem, with the additional disadvantage of an unfavourable natural background, must obviously remain in the forefront of all political concerns.

The Distribution of Land in 1949

Class	Number of families	Area owned			
		Percentage of total families	In millions of hectares	Per-centages	Average per family
Landed proprietors	2,400,000	4	44	50	18·2
Rich peasants	3,600,000	6	15·5	18	4·3
Moderately well-off peasants	12,000,000	20	13	15	1·1
Poor peasants and farm workers	42,000,000	70	14·4	17	0·3

It is clear from this table that property was extremely unevenly divided, and the holding of the average peasant barely large enough to provide for his needs. This problem which was fundamental in imperial China is well known to the Communist Party who, ever since their foundation in 1921, have wanted to put an end to such a wasteful economy with its inevitable condemnation of the peasant to permanent destitution. To Mao, 'The only means of putting an end to this situation is gradual collectivization; and, as Lenin taught, the only road to that lies by way of cooperation.' (*Selected Works*, Vol. IV). Thus, as 'liberation' of the provinces was gradually effected by the people's Red Army, agrarian reform would be established in two or three cantons, and then analysed. What was learnt from such analyses could then, like oil, gradually seep through the whole province. The slowness of this procedure was due to the fact that the essence of Maoist propaganda was first of all to get

*1 hectare = 100 ares, or 2·471 acres. 1 are = 100 square metres. 1 square metre = 1·196 square yards.

the peasants to grasp that their poverty was not something decreed by fate, but merely the consequence of the political situation. Therefore, though the 1921 revolution did not provide any solution to the agrarian problem (in fact the peasants' situation was actually worsened because of fighting between the 'warlords'), the advent of Mao was to lead to the most gigantic agrarian reform history has ever known.

The Peasant: an Unconscious Socialist

It was on 2 June 1950 that the law of agrarian reform was promulgated, bringing to an end a system that had existed for thousands of years. It satisfied the vast majority of the peasants to whom it gave pieces of land, and whose existing debts for rent were cancelled. So the peasant had suddenly become a small landowner (50 million hectares changed hands); 300 million poor peasants saw their bits of land increase, but given the minute size they were (5 to 10 ares), the lack of farming implements or working animals, the need for cooperation was implicit in the situation. A further step was then made with the 'Mutual Help' movement, which soon became a semi-socialist cooperative (communal use of tools, animals, etc.). The small landowner of 1950 was not to have the illusion of being a propertied man for long, for, from 1955, he was to become an agricultural worker in one of the 700,000 cooperatives (i.e., collective farms) created up and down the country. In 1958 he was no longer a farm worker but a fighter on the economic front established by the people's communes – the idea for which was put forward by the Peking daily (*Renmin Ribao*, 18 August 1958). Adopted on 29 August by the Communist Central Committee meeting at Peitaiho (but only made public on 10 September), the 'Decision to establish people's communes' – clear evidence of China's ambition to do faster and better what had been done in Russia – enforced the system on the whole of Chinese agriculture. From then on, the development of the people's communes proceeded rapidly.

As you see, then, development was so rapid as to bring about certain distortions, with the consequent need to make readjust-

Development of the Communes

1958	End of August	Mid-September	End of September	End of December
Number of communes	8,730	16,787	26,425	26,578
Number of families in communes	37,780,000	81,220,000	121,000,000	123,250,000
Percentage of peasant families in communes	30·4	65·3	98	99·1
Average number of families per commune	4,238	4,781	4,614	4,637

ments; in 1959, the 26,578 communes (which had taken over from the 700,000 cooperatives) had fallen to 24,000, each having on average 5,000 families (usually about 25,000 people); then, the initial units broke up, and there are now some 75,000. These 75,000 people's communes are subdivided into 700,000 smaller groups (really still the old cooperatives) and 4,800,000 work-teams, each working about 20 hectares. Thus the 'de-communized' people's commune was reduced to a more human scale. The work-teams (of 40–60 peasants) now collectively owned the land they worked, the working-animals, and all heavy machinery. They formed their plans for crops, divided out the labour, calculated the 'sections of work' (like the soviet *troudodien*): the system was complicated when it came to paying the workers, and gave rise to frequent recriminations.

Thus, it is the lower levels of the collectivist system that play the major part in China today, whereas in Russia the opposite is the case. The higher level is the people's commune, responsible for collective achievements requiring large investments – from canals to crèches, from silos to old people's homes – who shake up the old routines and try to 'reconstruct' the very thoughts of the peasants – who since the days of Hesiod have always been the most tenacious of all human groups. And it is within the people's communes that the Communist Party is organized in all the country areas. Unlike Russia, the people's commune constitutes the ultimate level of the State, since political administration and economic management are carried out by the same people. And to the Communist Party, it is in this that the people's commune is a success, for it thus makes it possible to keep control of the totality of the rural population. It is far easier for the party to direct 75,000 people's communes than 120 million families of peasants.

Thus, it took only three years (1955–8) for the Chinese Communist leaders to establish a collectivist system radically different from the Soviet pattern: collectivization in Russia took four years (1929–33) to achieve far less, and at the cost of a ghastly civil war (Churchill's memoirs record Stalin's admission that 10 million died) and the killing of about half the livestock by the rebel peasants (270 million altogether – horses, cattle, sheep and pigs – in 1928; 166 million three years later; as recorded in Stalin's report to the Seventeenth Party Congress, January 1934). Though the changeover to collectivization did not cost so much in China, there was still a rumbling discontent, expressed, especially in the centre and the south, by serious uprisings, though these were soon put down (the north remained more passive). Li Hsien-nien admitted: 'Tension reigned in country areas. . . . In places they even destroyed trees and crops, and killed pigs.'

But, as Mao has said:

Revolution is not a gala banquet; it can't be made like a literary work, a drawing or a piece of embroidery; it cannot be done with such elegance, such tranquillity and delicacy, nor with such gentleness, pleasantness and politeness, such restraint and generosity of spirit. Revolution is an uprising, an act of violence by which one class overthrows another . . .

Report on the Inquiry Made in Hunan on the Peasant Movement

Mao's initiative was bound to arouse violent opposition from the Russians, and this showed itself in three ways: ideologically (because the people's communes were a denial of Russia's monopoly in the transition to Communism), historically (because of the failure of the Soviet agricultural cooperatives after 1917), and economically (the Communist principle, said Moscow, could not be applied initially to rural situations). The uniqueness

– or the challenge – of Mao's agrarian reform was that by making the people's commune the basic cell of rural life, red China, despite the poverty of its communications is actually ahead of the West as it is going at present. Furthermore, this Maoist structure is equally extraordinary at the social level: as the basic unit of socialist society, the people's commune brings together workers, peasants, shopkeepers, soldiers and students, and thus effaces – or at least tries to efface – all the distinctions between the various categories of citizen, as well as between town and country. On the economic plane, the commune provides a framework for production; it is a means of getting the utmost out of local resources, and in addition makes use of the working force for 250 days in the year – instead of the 120–150 of pre-commune times – and also provides an effective control of consumption. Nor is the vital political aspect forgotten; the central authority lies in the hands of the Party committee in each commune, and its control can be seen in all areas. The Party makes the law and is a law unto itself. But it is perhaps at the military level that the commune is most singular: it can, in fact, deal with all the essential administrative, economic, social and political functions. Having in addition a militia (recruited from among former soldiers, peasants, workers, students and party members) it forms a complete unit for survival in case of nuclear war. It is furthermore in a position to establish a guerrilla army all over the country were there to be a foreign invasion. Though the people's commune has undeniable advantages, it must be admitted that they are dearly paid for: in this Communist 'climate', the peasant has lost all freedom (of time, of work, of methods used in growing, crops chosen for planting, etc.); he no longer belongs to his family, but is wholly at the service of the State – the commune's employer. The result is that the Chinese peasant is hedged in as never before.

Campaign for Production

It is quite clear, though Europe seems not to realize the fact, that in the future we shall see, and be unable to prevent, the

disappearance of traditional peasant societies in face of technological progress and the needs of the State. It is perhaps worth
noting that it is red China, a country still technologically backward, which has given birth to the most daring new structures.
But will the Chinese peasant, who is paying the bill, so to speak,
stand for it? It is a question he answers simply by his work: the
material results are self-explanatory. And yet, there again, one
must never forget the legacy of the past: the basically agricultural population of China have been accustomed since the dawn
of history to such rural communities in which life is rigidly
disciplined; the mentality of life in common is part of their
makeup.

So the battle for production has been won, despite the rigours
it has enforced. But sacrifices and efforts have not been demanded in vain, for the Chinese people have at last emerged
from the appalling destitution in which they have lived for
centuries: the collectivity is now stronger and more prosperous
than it ever was in the past.

By its conversion to Communism twenty years ago, China
may well have actually taken the quickest road to becoming a
modern state. Obviously the income of a family of farm workers
in a people's commune will vary according to the number of
members who are working (and also their income from private
bits of land, and such home-made goods as sweaters or baskets),
and the area where the commune is situated (rich or poor
districts). However, the improvement in the standard of living
is satisfactory, and can be seen everywhere: it is clear from
savings (deposits in the savings bank of the commune) and even
that primitive form of saving represented by stocks of rice or
cereals kept near the bed of the master of the house; and there
are such other signs of wealth as bicycles, wristwatches, and
above all the Thermos, so essential for keeping water (not tea)
hot. It is wonderful to see how proudly, and with what touching
courtesy and spontaneity, these peasants will bring you into
their tiny homes for a drink of hot water, and some bread and
pimento.

Yet no picture, however perfect, is without its flaws, and in
this case natural disasters have provided them. The harvest of

1960 was one of the worst in the revolution's history, and the threat of starvation made the authorities order the planting of every scrap of land that could be cultivated at all – courtyards, pavements, embankments, everything – while at the same time establishing the most rigid rationing. Also, the supreme concession: from December 1960, the right, recently suppressed, was restored for individuals to cultivate a piece of land near the farm, and proportionate in size to the number in each family: the total of such individual allotments must not, however, exceed 5 per cent of the area worked by the commune collectively. Individual raising of animals (goats, chickens, sheep, pigs, etc.) was restored and in fact positively encouraged. Such concessions, known as 'little freedoms', though for the moment necessary and advantageous to the national economy, were strictly temporary, and in no way suggested an abandonment of the collective principle.

The fact that the regime survived the three black years (1959–61) in which natural conditions had damaged harvests to an unprecedented degree, proved to the Chinese that Heaven had not withdrawn its mandate, its 'divine commission', from the 'Red Emperor', Mao, that man of outstanding fertility of mind, but also of rigidity and endless contradictions. And the disasters *were* overcome. There are no more of the horrible famines (such as that in 1920–21, when half a million people died, and ten million were left destitute). There are no more appalling diseases of crops or livestock (with 12 million tons of cereals, or 8 per cent of the total production, 15 per cent of the total livestock, 20 per cent of the pigs, 30 per cent of the chickens lost every year). Mao had fought the Dragons, and won.

Though all too often peasants still push swing-ploughs in the rice-fields as they did under the Ming – while Peking has the H-bomb – it remains true that China's agriculture is continually improving, through the vast efforts of innumerable workers. They re-afforest (about 20 million hectares), drain and irrigate (about 60 million). Day by day the agronomic laboratories are using their research to support scientific, rational and productive agricultural methods.

The year 1967, with better weather conditions than any since the beginning of the People's Republic, should have produced a record harvest. Yet, by an irony of fate, no record exists for that year – the very year of the 'Cultural Revolution' whose whole purpose was to 'stimulate production'. Except for those within 50 kilometres of the cities, people in country areas were barely touched by the turmoil of the 'Cultural Revolution'. Nevertheless, there were places where the relaxation of political and administrative controls was seized on by the peasants as an occasion for dividing up amongst themselves not only the collective reserves of cereals, but also the seeds destined for the commune, and for giving more time to their private allotments or other individual work (basket-making, for instance). Indeed the situation appeared so grave that Mao issued a personal directive (*Renmin Ribao*, 16 and 23 September 1967) on 'Six good tactics to pursue': good production, good harvest, good choice of seeds, good food supplies, good division, good stocks for the future. Ultimately the problems arising out of the 'Cultural Revolution' remained localized – the peasants remaining outside political struggles unlike the young people and workers – and the agricultural advance seems hardly to have been slowed down at all.

Development of Land Production

Years	Land-area, in millions of hectares	Kilos produced per hectare	Total yield in millions of tons
1957	118·8	1,448	172
1962	118·8	1,515	180
1963	118·5	1,502	178
1964	120·5	1,577	190
1965	120·8	1,531	185
1966	120	1,483	178
1967	120	1,558	187

Imports of cereals have also gone down since 1964: that year they reached a record of 6·4 million tons, in 1965 6 million, in 1966 5·5 million, and in 1967 4·3 million. Peking maintains them at a certain level to help to feed the numbers of people concentrated in coastal areas where enough food cannot be produced, thus lightening the burden on internal transport, which is already hard put to it to cope with the needs of industry. At the same time, the country is exporting more rice (500,000 tons in 1964; a million in 1967). To import a certain amount also means setting free part of the labour force (and of the country's capital) for industry. Harvests will always be subject to the whims of nature, and even by 1968 the future looked less bright. In point of fact, weather in the winter of 1967–8 was none too good, and the winter cereal crop (one fifth of the world's total production) suffered. Then the first rice crop was badly flooded, bringing a lower harvest than usual (12 per cent down in Kwangtung province) and delaying the sowing of the second crop, so that it too was under par. At the same time, the northern regions were subjected to a drought in the spring of 1968. Apart from some fundamental change in the natural and political climate, no remarkable alteration could be expected before 1970, the third year of the present five-year plan. The virtues of the old China (intensive farming has been perfected almost from the beginning, and the Chinese peasant is the most courageous in the world), and efficient organization (cadres, indoctrination, and organization brought in by the Communist Party) have combined to give people's China considerable success in matters agricultural.

A Warning Signal

Though the agricultural balance sheet after twenty years of Communist rule looks, by and large, favourable, people's China with its basically rural physiognomy (80 per cent of the population living in the country) still remains an underdeveloped nation with almost unlimited needs. This I think no one doubts. Certainly not the authorities in Peking. Thus, though mechanization has made considerable strides, it is still in its early stages. People's China at present has only something in the region of 50,000 tractors, where a million are needed. Machinery for irrigation still falls far short of what is required. The nutritive content to be got from commercial fertilizers has now reached about eight kilos per hectare of arable land; in Great

Britain twenty-five times that quantity of fertilizer is used; in Japan, forty times! As for natural manure – used for thousands of years – it would take five years to integrate it into the production processes. Millions of good fields are still unused; but to reclaim them all – though this began to be done in 1956 – would call for a degree of mechanization and an amount of money that seems quite beyond present possibilities.

Agriculture, then, still needs innumerable pumps, tractors, drainage pipes, and fertilizers – all things that can only be produced by heavy industry. So Peking is inevitably forced to give that priority. The definite reversal – agriculture the basic sector, industry the dominant factor – seems a neat enough formula. And indeed, by creating the myth of agriculture, by giving agricultural work back its old prestige, by sending young party cadres to settle in the country, Peking is preventing the rightly dreaded migration of tens of millions of country-people to the cities. However, while stressing the supreme role of agriculture, the Communist authorities, as will become clear later on, demonstrate in everything they do the greater importance given to heavy industry. Despite all its inadequacies, Chinese agriculture is continually producing more and more. People's China, twenty years after the largest-scale agricultural reform ever undertaken anywhere, does not merely manage to feed its own swarming population (with a 2 per cent increase each year), but actually produces more than they need, and can export a considerable amount of foodstuffs.

Peking's unique experiment thus presents the hungry masses of Asia and Africa with a compelling example, as they struggle to find some way out of their own underdevelopment. And certainly, those countries which depend solely on the aid they may get from Europe – whose standards of comfort they also accept – without demanding efforts from their own people, will never make any progress. The Chinese example is clear evidence that effort by the people on the spot in matters agricultural is far and away the most essential basis for development.

Though it is obviously difficult to provide a precise diagnosis of a contemporary political situation, since it is an essentially fluid thing, it would certainly be a mistake not to see the

Chinese agricultural challenge as the warning sign of a radical change in the conditions of production and international economics. It is essential therefore that the West pay serious attention to the nature of the Chinese challenge – not losing sight of the fact that even now the 5 per cent growth rate in Western economy is outpaced by one of 7 per cent in the Eastern, socialist countries: awareness of this now may save us from a painful awakening in the future.

B. AN INDUSTRY IN PROPORTION TO THE COUNTRY

Only forty-five years have passed since the 1911 revolution, and today the whole face of China is totally different. In another forty-five years, in 2001, as we enter the twenty-first century, China will have seen further, even more important changes. It will have become a powerful socialist industrialized country.

Mao Tse-tung

China as an agricultural nation, no longer destitute, prepared to withstand famine, secure against disasters, with every day's bowl of rice assured, can only prosper if it goes hand in hand with China as an industrial nation. But the Chinese leaders did not have the chance to try out their programme and methods on the centres of industry that they had in the spheres of political structures and agrarian reform; for after the bloody defeats of Shanghai and Canton in 1927, they were repelled, and only got back there in 1948–9.

The industrial 'revolution' poses completely different problems, and solutions appropriate to them are continually being sought. The solutions demanded would embrace both the positive and negative contributions of the Chinese experiment to the theory and practice of Marxism in this continent-State, the first country to have achieved socialism while starting from so low a level of industry.

The pages that follow will therefore suggest a summing-up – only approximate, alas – of the industrial story, for a detailed study of each sector is virtually impossible due to the lack of statistical information.

I have had to put forward a certain number of hypotheses. But despite all the obstacles, it is not hypothesis but fact that, starting from nothing, people's China has, in twenty years, become a major industrial power, and intends in the future to play an active part in the world.

The Problem of Foreigners

Before Marco Polo discovered that the China he had visited was far ahead of thirteenth-century Europe, its mining industry already had a long and splendid history. Under the Chou dynasty, for instance, they had a metal coinage; under the Han (202 B.C.–A.D. 220), they mined coal, the 'black stones one can burn like brushwood' that so surprised the traveller from Venice; from time immemorial, the major metals had been known and used in China. So it was historical development, rather than any inadequacy in resources, that made Chinese industry in the twentieth century so inferior to that in the West: the sad fact was that, vast though they were, all possibilities for development were subordinated to economic interests which were not those of the Chinese people. Imperialist influence in China seems to have aimed mainly at supplying raw materials to the industry of developed countries at attractive prices. The pride of the subjects of an Empire which from early times had received tribute from its neighbours – an application of Confucian teaching to foreign affairs – could not but be stung by contact with those 'foreign devils' (this contemptuous term, *Yang Kueitzu*, was officially abolished in 1870) who by placing their country under regular taxation from the opium war to the Boxer uprising, seemed to be doing everything possible to merit such a title.

Of course, China was never totally taken over by the Western powers, but pieces of Chinese territory were subject to concessions to other countries, monstrous though such legislation was. Foreigners came to play a totally crushing role in the country's economic life: duties and taxes were controlled by the

British, the postal services were in the hands of the French and 65 per cent of China's trade was still controlled by the British and Japanese as late as 1930; all the Chinese banks put together owned less than the four big British banks, while half of China's coal production and 45 per cent of its textile factories were in the hands of foreign firms.

Foreign investments might one day have been of advantage to China had they been so distributed as to form a well-balanced infrastructure. But that they were not: 40·5 per cent of industry was concentrated in the Shanghai area, 33·7 per cent in Manchuria and 25·8 per cent in the rest of the country. In short, Shanghai and Manchuria formed the industrial centre of gravity, while the rest of China was almost totally without modern industry of any kind. Thus the presence and the encroachments of foreigners, mainly Westerners, as Mao said, made China 'a semi-colonial country'.

'Building the Foundations'

The economic strategy of the new Government established in Peking, once again the capital city (every new dynasty always made a point of choosing a new capital, and Mao was careful to keep the tradition going), was dominated by two objectives: first, to break totally with the economic infrastructure of Chiang Kai-chek, which was made all the easier by ten years of corruption and the fact that the masses were wholly behind the Communists; and secondly, to create a planned economy, as dictated by Marxist doctrine, giving absolute priority to heavy industry, followed by light industry, and lastly by agriculture. This recovery of the economy covers the period from 1949 to 1952, which saw the complete reform of agriculture and, in the industrial sector, a slow process of socialization which, by transforming existing structures, achieved a genuine industrial revolution built round three key ideas: gradual socialization (industries, banks, businesses); priority for heavy industry (coal, steel, machinery) with about 83 per cent of all investment, as compared with 17 per cent in light industry which was to be organized on a local level (provinces, people's communes) rather than on a national one; and the creation of new industrial centres (in the north-east and in central China) together with an appeal to local initiative to make the best possible use of the labour force and all local resources. However, the Communist leaders were not lacking in common sense, and their intention was openly stated: to leave the capitalists where they were until such time as the State was equipped to do without them.*

The time then came to move on to the next stage of the 'economy of the new democracy': nationalizations, seizures and expulsions now struck foreign firms, as the State gradually took over railways, banks, industries (heavy and light), businesses (wholesale, retail and foreign). Thus, the State's share in modern industry, which in terms of production reached 34·2 per cent in 1949, continued growing until it was 99·6 per cent in 1956, thus involving 98 per cent of all blue- and white-collar workers. Campaigns expressively known as 'tiger hunts' prepared to eliminate methodically all private enterprise: from being 63·3 per cent of the whole in 1949, their share in the Chinese economy fell to 24·9 per cent in 1954, and two years later that too was transformed into State enterprise. The minister Li Fu-chun could state categorically that in 1959 the private sector (in industry, artisanship and commerce) provided a mere one per cent of all production.† Needless to say, all these steps inevitably provoked reactions and indeed positive hostility which might well prove a danger to the new regime. Henceforth, repression was unavoidable. Meanwhile, the Korean war saw the entry into action on 25 October 1950 of 'Chinese people's volunteers', in the guise of 'The Movement of Resistance to America and Assistance to Korea': to protect one's neighbour is to protect oneself. For the first time, after over a century of humiliations, the Chinese armies were holding back American soldiers – America then being the only nation to possess the atom bomb – and actually forcing them to retreat. Ultimately, the Korean war did the regime more good than harm for, by striking a nationalist and anti-American chord in all hearts, it provided a splendid opportunity to speed up the pace of the 'revolution', and to

* cf. Mao Tse-tung; *On Popular Democratic Dictatorship*, 30 June 1949.
† Report to the National Assembly, 21 April 1959.

impose draconian measures for internal security. The fact that the Chinese intervention in Korea was designated as a 'Movement' also indicates something of its significance for the internal situation. In any case, repression clamped down on public opinion, and any Chinese who did not feel called to be a martyr steered clear of trouble.

Despite the direct, indirect and cumulative effects of the Korean war, the period of reconstruction reached its end in 1952. People's China by then was, *mutatis mutandis*, in the situation Russia had been in in 1927, in other words the best years of the New Economic Policy.

Russia in 1927 Compared with China in 1952

	Unit	Russia 1927	China 1952
Population	millions	147	583
Industrial workers – blue- and white-collar	millions	4·1	4
Land under cultivation	millions of hectares	112·4	108
Coal	millions of tons	32·3	63·8
Iron	millions of tons	3	1·9
Steel	millions of tons	3·7	1·3
Electricity	millions of kWh.	4,205	7,260
Cement	thousands of tons	1,403	2,860
Railway lines	thousands of km.	75·6	24·2

These figures are taken from S. Adler: *The Chinese Economy*, London, 1957.

The Chinese results were all the more astounding, in that the country was starting from so much lower a level. China, having by now returned roughly to the same level as in 1943, its previous high point, the Communist leaders considered the country to be sufficiently secure to impose a rigid framework upon its economy. When the first five-year plan was put into operation on 1 January 1953, the policy of the socialist transformation of industry, officially adopted in March 1949, began to be applied in practice. Then began the 'glorious historic task of building the foundations of the nation'. This cry, first launched in 1952, was for years to remain a leitmotiv of national propaganda; what it meant was the building of a sound, diversified and planned economy on a solid basis. One phase, the special phase, was over and was giving way to the constructive phase: since, of its essence, the Maoist revolution is in a continual state of evolution, each of its phases must, by definition, be transitory.

Getting off the Ground Economically

The first five-year plan (1953-7), according to the official literature, was to lay the foundations of socialist industrialization. The economy overrode all other considerations. China was, during that first five years, to achieve remarkable results in every area, though the Chinese planners appeared rather too concerned with building up a vast industry, by channelling into it most of the investments needed especially by light industry and by agriculture. The Peking official daily gives this account of the successes achieved by the first five-year plan, and gives the word for the future:

... The total value of industrial production is 17·3 per cent higher than the goal set by the first five-year plan, thus representing an increase of 132·5 per cent over 1952. Steel production reached 5,240,000 tons; coal, 128,000,000 tons; cast iron, 5,900,000 tons; electricity, 19,000,000,000 kilowatts; cotton, 4,610,000 bales. Cereal production reached 185,000,000 tons, even higher than in 1956. Thanks to the party leadership, the hard work of the whole people, and the aid of the U.S.S.R. and other sister-nations, our first five-year plan has succeeded beyond all expectations. However, the achievement of that first plan is only a beginning. It will probably take another ten to fifteen years to lay the foundations for modern industry and agriculture in our country. We want to equal, if not surpass, Great Britain in fifteen years in the production of steel and other major industrial products; after that, we shall devote another twenty or thirty years in continuing to increase productivity with a view to equalling and overtaking the U.S.A.'s economy, and gradually leading China from being a socialist society to being a communist society. That is the glorious and arduous historical task of the Chinese people.

Renmin Ribao, 1 January 1968

A comparison of how China's gross industrial production was divided at the end of the first five-year plan with that of other countries speaks for itself.

Comparison with Other Countries in 1957

Percentage in 1957	U.S.A.	France	Japan	U.S.S.R.	India	China
Agriculture and stock-breeding	6·4	15	23·4	24·1	56·4	48·3
Industry and construction	59·2	63	48·6	59·7	22·6	36·4
Services (transport, shops, etc.)	34·4	22	28	16·2	21	15·3

These figures are taken from the U.N. Statistical Yearbooks.

We see at once that almost half of China's gross internal production rises out of agricultural activities, which then provided a living for 85 per cent of the population, at that time some 550 million Chinese. India, whose economy follows capitalist principles, and respects the traditional values of the country, is clearly underdeveloped. Now in 1952 the two countries had very similar structures. Five years later, China had overtaken India in basic industry (steel, coal, electricity). Yet China's rate of growth in 1957, though far from inconsiderable, was held to be quite inadequate by Mao, who had adopted the Soviet pattern in the hope of achieving a far more rapid development which would soon make the new China the dominant power in Asia. Therefore, China's economic development must follow not the criteria of the industrial socialist countries, but its own Chinese methods.

A Political and Socio-economic Whirlwind

At the end of the first five-year plan, people's China was none the less in a somewhat paradoxical situation: a modern industrial sector employing only 8 per cent of the active labour force, was absorbing about half of all economic investments, while an agricultural sector employing over 80 per cent of the active labour force was receiving only 12 per cent of the total investment, and, furthermore, actually forced to finance the investment in the modern industrial sector!

The Chinese leaders therefore asked that all Russia's foreign aid should be given to them. Moscow refused politely. For important reasons of international politics and strategy, Moscow intended to continue giving aid to non-Communist countries (especially India and Egypt). Furthermore, the problems Russia was having with the aftermath of the Polish troubles and the Hungarian uprising, forced it actually to decrease the aid it was giving to China. It may be that Moscow also feared too rapid a growth on the part of its only possible rival in the Communist world.

The Chinese grasped that they must work out their own pattern, and not continue slavishly following the Soviet model. Suddenly the 'good pupil' attitude, which had characterized the years 1953–7, disappeared, and was replaced by a new Sinization of economic ideas. Mao, more disappointed than he would ever admit, made bold innovations, rejecting the Soviet pattern of economic development, and with the 'Great Leap Forward' involved the whole mass of the people in the work of production, launching China into an experiment unparalleled in the modern world. Whatever he may have said, Mao's real concern was with heavy industry, and though he did not give up the idea of forming vast collectives in the Soviet fashion, he was bent on enlarging the industrial sector by appealing to a fresh source of capital: not investment, or machinery, or technicians, but the mass of the people.

A new slogan suddenly appeared (the use of slogans is a long-standing Chinese tradition): 'Walking on two feet', to express the intention of the Peking leaders that the country's economic development should be supported by both the industrial and the agricultural sectors. The mass campaign for iron and steel, together with the campaign for the people's communes, was to turn the whole country upside down. But I cannot warn my readers too strongly against seeing only the weaknesses in the Great Leap Forward – described by Chou En-lai as 'a better road to building socialism'.* For it is incontestable that in a

* Speech to the National Assembly, 18 April 1959.

year China succeeded in doubling its output of cast iron and steel, thus at a bound becoming one of the major iron-producing countries of the world. The little village blast-furnaces – rudimentary, built of bricks and clay, often totally unequipped – may have had no more than a propaganda value, but the real little blast furnaces (of six to thirty cubic metres) made it possible for country-people, who had up to then only handled the most elementary of tools, to understand something of the importance of industry. It was those little furnaces that produced the cast iron from which the workshops and small factories made the tools the peasants must have in order to respond to the campaign for increased farm production.

The Great Leap Forward used more than 500 million pairs of hands for its vast-scale works of irrigation, flood control, and road-building to provide transport for the steel industry. The Great Leap Forward was a stimulant to every sector of China's economy, and an amount of effort unparalleled in the West went into great building programmes – factories, estates for workers, public buildings, major public works. For instance, in 1958, 150,000 kilometres of roads were built, more than during the whole of the first five-year plan. In that same year, 80,000 small mines were developed – and, despite their small size, among them they produced a quarter of the country's total coal production of 270 million tons. The foundations were laid for creating a steel industry in every province of China. And the production of steel leapt up fantastically, growing from 5,350,000 tons to 11,080,000 tons in a year (and that does not include the 'people's steel'). 'Produce more, faster, better, and cheaper' was a slogan which distilled neatly the inspiration of the Great Leap Forward, and it was one that was heard and acted upon by the mass of the people.

But in the end this tremendous rush of energy on the part of both workers and machines wore them out. No amount of revolutionary fervour can transcend the sheer physical limits of any human activity. The Great Leap Forward, by attempting more than the country could achieve, created tensions: these were exacerbated by poor harvests (due both to natural disasters and to the establishment of the people's communes – a new departure, involving the mistakes inseparable from the untried) and, worse still, led to the withdrawal of Soviet aid. (Peking has never recognized any other cause for the failure of the Great Leap Forward apart from this and the poor harvests.) The cereal crops, so vital for feeding the country, fell from 190 to 155 million tons. The gross national product fell by 32 per cent between 1960 and 1961. So the whole policy of out-and-out industrialization inspired by the promethean spirit of Mao was brought into doubt. Liu Shao-chi, Mao's second-in-command, and other 'realist' party members set their faces against the whole thing, and tried to force Mao to yield his position as President and retain only the spiritual leadership of the party.

The Central Committee of the party met at Wuhan from 28 November to 10 December 1959, and introduced a certain prudence and sense of proportion. In the course of its communiqués, we read: '. . . It is necessary to try to establish economic planning on a secure basis, and to maintain the right balance among our various objectives, in harmony with the objective law of the proportional development of the different sectors of the national economy. . . . In economics, one must show prudence, and act, if not wholly, then as far as possible, in conformity with the realities.' Responsibility for both economic policy and propaganda passed into the hands of the pragmatists, and Liu Shao-chi emerged as not merely Mao's successor-designate, but as already his equal in power and importance. Liu certainly had good cause to produce a new edition of his book, *How to be a Good Communist* (the Chinese title means, literally, 'Achieving self-perfection'), with the addition of a condemnation of 'those who think themselves the Marx and Lenin of China'. And he closes with a question which, after ten years, is particularly striking: 'Can we be certain that people of that kind will no longer rise to the head of our party? No, we cannot.'

For the moment, people's China returned to less adventurous and more classic norms of development in the industrial sphere: instead of a Great Leap Forward, there was to be a regular pace . . .

'Develop by Our Own Strength'

The Chinese industrial challenge was not well received at the Kremlin, and during the summer of 1960, Khrushchev's stopping of Soviet aid, recalling of Russian experts, cancelling of contracts and abandonment of plans for cooperation, were to be a hard blow to the Chinese economy. This particular 'eternal' friendship had lasted just ten years.

So China was alone. Soviet machinery must at once be replaced by machinery made in China, substitutes must be found for commodities from such socialist countries as East Germany and Czechoslovakia, cereals would have to be bought from the imperialist world, and, the biggest problem of all, technicians must be trained. Peking was forced to clutch at every straw – hence the Chinese leaders' cries of 'treason' to Russia. All their plans had to be reviewed: industry would have to go more slowly, and the Government in Peking thus found themselves forced to move backwards politically – euphemistically described as 'readjustment'.

This about-face was accompanied by a new policy embodied in the order to 'develop by our own strength', a phrase which, it is important to realize, had a double meaning. The first related to general economic policy: China must develop her economy by her own powers, that is by embarking on plans for investment that could be achieved with the technical means then at her disposal. This did not, of course, mean an autarchic orientation of the national economy: China was not trying to be self-sufficient in everything, and certainly was far from totally abandoning foreign trade. In fact, as will be seen in the next chapter, Chinese foreign trade was to be systematically expanded. In its second meaning the phrase was an appeal to every individual unit of production to try to achieve as much as it possibly could without asking for help from the State; in other words, every enterprise must manage with as little financial demand on the State as possible, and try to increase production by new methods, or by improving its old plant. Thus the chief effort was being asked of the workers themselves.

More than at any other time in the history of the development of Chinese socialism, stress was laid on the political conscience whereby material stimuli must be made to play a relatively minor role; a new socialist attitude was created in which work must be treated no longer as an activity to which one is condemned in order to earn a living, but as an activity worthwhile in itself, an enrichment for everyone. Consumption must no longer, as in capitalist countries, be the sole purpose of human activity – indeed it must be seen as a new form of alienation (the subjection of man to things, the never-satisfied need to consume): in China, man must find his real purpose in creating, not in consuming . . .

To return to our story, I should point out that the year 1962 should, in theory, have been the last year of the second five-year plan (1958–62), but that plan – which was never in fact published – really only existed as an idea from 1960 onwards. Though, therefore, the third plan was supposed to be determining the Chinese economy from 1 January 1963, it was continually delayed. During 1963 and 1964, harvests were good. The reorganization of the economy had also borne fruit, and, on the admission of Chou En-lai himself, by 1964 the production level had once again reached what it was before the Great Leap Forward. We know for a fact that the G.N.P. achieved in 1957 was even, in some sectors, surpassed in 1964.

Levels of Production in 1957 and 1964

Product	Unit	1957	1964
Coal	millions of tons	130	215
Crude oil	millions of tons	1·5	7·2
Steel	millions of tons	5·3	10
Cement	millions of tons	5·6	9·7
Chemical fertilizers	millions of tons	0·8	3·5
Natural gas	millions of m³	600	
Electricity	thousands of millions of kWh.	22	36
Lorries		7,500	25,000
Cattle	millions	62	65
Pigs	millions	102	150
Cereals	millions of tons	172	190

So, the period of regression (1961–2), marked by a catastrophic fall in agricultural production (following on the three 'black years' of 1959–61) together with a fall in industrial production, was followed by a period of rapid expansion (1963–4) – particularly in the sectors of power and heavy industry (steel, iron, mining): marking the success of an economic manoeuvre designed to give priority to sectors of 'strategic' importance, from both the economic and the military point of view. The satisfactory expansion of both power and heavy industry confirmed the view that planning leads to rapid progress. And the more modest advance in light industry and consumer goods was the result of a policy designed to increase investment as against consumption. The crisis following the Great Leap Forward was over. But the seeds of a further crisis had already been sown – this time a political one – and they flowered into the Cultural Revolution of 1966. Since the spring of 1964, Marshal Lin Piao (who had replaced Marshal Peng Teh-huai as Minister of Defence in September 1959) had filled the major administrative and business posts in industry with his own men, while putting Chiang Ching (Mrs Mao) in charge of the 'cultural' section of the army. Hence, it was inevitable that Lin Piao's team would have to confront the rival party team led by the president, Liu Shao-chi, and the secretary-general of the party, Teng Hsiao-ping. American escalation in Vietnam proved exceptionally helpful to the marshal. What happened was that when the bombing of North Vietnam began on 2 March 1965, Khrushchev's successors (it was now six months since his downfall), suggested to Peking that they form a 'united front' against the Americans. Once again the Chinese leaders were divided. Those who wanted to accept Russia's advances – the President, the Commander-in-chief of the armed forces, General Lo Jui-ching, and their supporters – found themselves in opposition to those who were at one with Mao and Lin Piao in the conviction that Russia would never risk a nuclear confrontation with America for the sake of North Vietnam, and then perhaps China. So the Soviet overtures were categorically rejected. Once again China stood alone. The whole country must be geared to stand against the threat of American invasion. Marshal Lin

Piao, in an article of immense length on 2 September 1965, 'Long Live the People's War, the Revolutionary War', sketched out the principles and rules governing a 'people's war'. However, when it came to foreign policy, despite a tremendous verbal slanging-match with the Americans, the Chinese exercised a policy of extreme prudence towards the United States – and actions, as we know, speak louder than words. Meanwhile at home, they were laying the ground for a total reorganization of their political and economic structures. In such a situation it would hardly have been possible to set the third five-year plan on foot in 1965.

The Cultural Revolution: a Tragedy of Underdevelopment

When it was at last launched, on 1 January 1966, the third five-year plan looked more like a statement of intention than a real plan, for no figures were published at all. However, the priorities established after the Great Leap Forward were maintained: agriculture as the basic sector, and industry as the dominant factor. But it soon appeared that the Peking authorities did not agree as to the lessons to be drawn from the Great Leap Forward; it could clearly lead in two possible – and opposite – directions: rectification or consolidation, in other words, a radical change or a continuation on the same lines, which would call for a new move towards socialization.

In the event, what happened was the Cultural Revolution – a tragic phenomenon of underdevelopment – whose rumblings could have been sensed as early as 1964. This movement, which André Malraux, in his *Anti-memoirs*,* describes as 'one of the most enormous psychological experiments ever made by man', by giving politics priority over the economy, was to condemn as traitors, counter-revolutionaries, 'black dragons' or 'foreign lackeys', everyone who asked questions, who argued, who doubted. Industrial production, now in full expansion once again, was stopped short by the upheavals of the Cultural Revolution. It burst upon industry in the early months of 1967 and hampered output (by work stoppages, changing the

*London, 1968.

function of factories, bloody incidents between rival groups); at the same time it created problems of transport which had the result of making deliveries late if not impossible, and food supplies in particular became uncertain since the movement of produce suffered more than most things. But though it did slow down production, the Cultural Revolution did not really disorganize the country's economy: there were troubles in a number of major industrial centres (especially Wuhan and Anshan where half the nation's steel comes from) but coming in the middle of a movement of expansion which had been constant since 1964, they merely slowed it down. The table overleaf seems to provide the best illustration of what I have been saying.

Thus, while owing to the highly selective nature of the industrial programme, remarkable advances were made in certain sectors (coal, oil, atomic power, heavy industry, textiles, sugar, the arms industry), certain other sectors were practically stagnant, especially light industries, because of their dependence on the development of production and the income from agriculture, and consumer goods. But since people's China had the foresight to create from the very first the fundamental conditions for economic growth, it is not impossible that, if stability is restored following the upheavals of the Cultural Revolution when, as the Chinese say, politics superseded economics, industry should soon rally, and recover its annual growth-rate of 8·5 per cent. After all, the fifty years of Communism's history have included periods of stagnation and economic recession, but also extraordinary spurts.

It remains true, however, that the varied and rapid expansion in its industrial development, which has brought such profound changes in the social sphere (development of the proletariat, the new female labour force), and even in the geographical nature of the country (landscapes changed, new industrial centres, workers' estates, factories, a move to colonize the west, and movements from the coast to the interior, right in to Sinkiang), could also turn China quite rapidly into a major industrial power.

Development in Various Branches of Industry

Sectors	1937	1952	1957	1962	1964	1966	1967		1970
							estimated	actual	estimated
Electrical power (millions of kWh.)	5,960	7,300	19,300	30,000	36,000	50,000	55,000	47,000	70,000
Coal (thousands of tons)	58,000	16,500	130,700	180,000	215,000	250,000	275,000	234,000	350,000
Crude oil (thousands of tons)	320	400	1,500	5,300	7,200	8,000	9,000	7,650	11,000
Steel (thousands of tons)	900	1,300	5,300	8,000	10,000	12,000	13,500	11,000	16,000
Chemical fertilizers (thousands of tons)	230	200	800	2,120	3,500	5,500	6,000	5,000	7,500
Cement (thousands of tons)	2,200	2,900	5,600	6,000	9,700	10,000	11,000	9,000	14,000
Cotton cloth (millions of metres)	2,790	3,800	5,000	3,000	3,600	4,000	4,500	4,000	6,000

Horizon for 1980

China's industry, which in the past few years has grown almost as fast as Japan's, can in fact look to the future with some confidence. There is certainly a vast territory in need of every kind of basic equipment: the railways are pitiably inadequate, and what there are of them are so concentrated as to be of little use to the west and the south; the roads are poor; the network of waterways is not evenly distributed, nor are the sources of raw materials; and, worst of all, any attempt to improve matters comes up against a vast mass of consumers impeding any accumulation of capital, and an industrial development depending mainly on agriculture. On the other hand, these disadvantages are counterbalanced by certain extremely favourable factors: China has more sources of raw materials than any other country in Asia; and the workers of China are easy to train, with a tradition of being both skilled and hard-working. Furthermore, China is entering an age that is far more advanced technologically than Japan entered in 1868 in the Meiji era, or Russia in 1928, the last year of the New Economic Policy. We are not going to be too wide of the mark if we say that what the Peking regime achieved in the industrial sphere during the first twenty years of its existence is enough to give us good reason for thinking that in its second twenty (and Mao was right, in the text I put at the head of this section, in suggesting a period of about forty years) China will become the third largest industrial power in the world. Perhaps, somewhere around the beginning of the next century, it will have become the largest.

If we are to attempt a long-term forecast – say the next ten years – based on the tendencies of the Chinese economy during the first five-year plan, we should, at the most optimistic, expect to see a great industrial expansion (8·34 per cent per year) and a smaller, but still large expansion of agricultural production (6·77 per cent). If we take this optimum as a basis, then the total net output* should increase on average by 7·66

*The term 'output' refers to the gross production of a given sector, allowing for all the purchases (raw materials, and so on) that have been needed to achieve that production. The sum total of such expenditure on material goods and services for that particular production is the 'input'.

per cent per year. But if we take a lower level of investment, with a lower proportion of industrial investment allotted to heavy industry – a more pessimistic forecast – then the expansion of the industrial sector will be less (6·17 per cent), and so will that of agriculture (5·74 per cent). In this case, the total output would only increase by 5·45 per cent per year – the lower limit of China's two-pronged economic development. Thus the economy would develop along a line somewhere between the first and second possibilities (cf. table and graph). For the

Economic Growth Assessment

(in thousands of millions of yuan. 1 yuan = 0·42 dollars)

	1957	1962	1967	1972	1977	1982	Average annual growth-rate
1st Assessment							
Net output of the industrial sector (organized sector)	52·91	77·94	114·97	172·33	261·64	391·96	8·34%
Net output of agriculture	38·52	52·45	72·99	99·73	143·91	197·91	6·77%
Total net output	111·02	156·67	221·28	313·64	460·61	659·60	7·37%
2nd Assessment							
Net output of the industrial sector	52·91	71·01	96·45	138·99	175·87	236·35	6·17%
Net output of agriculture	38·52	53·65	69·17	89·80	113·86	145·90	5·47%
Total net output	111·02	146·26	190·64	247·36	321·19	417·98	5·45%

Possible Extent of the Development of the Chinese Economy from 1957 to 1982

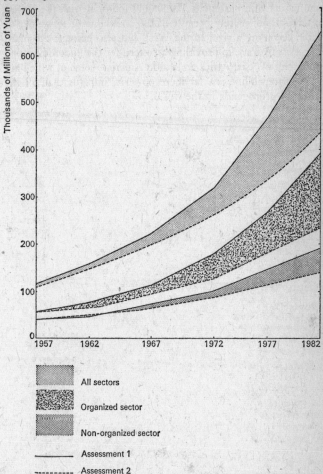

* The 'organized sector' is the sector in which production is carried out by the use of modern techniques, and directly controlled by the planners – in short the generalized sector known as secondary, or industrial.

The 'non-organized sector' is the sector in which production is carried out by traditional techniques – in other words the primary or agricultural sector.

present, at any rate, the effort to develop Chinese industry is in the nature of a challenge. We should follow it with the closest attention, not merely because of the possibility of its sooner or later becoming a rival to the West, but also because the rapid success of China, in providing a pattern for the underdeveloped countries of Asia, Africa and Latin America, some of which are our responsibility, is a far more powerful impetus than all the political propaganda in the world.

THREE. THE COMMERCIAL CHALLENGE

We want to do business, and business will always be done. We are not against anybody, apart from those reactionaries both inside and outside the country who prevent our doing business.

Mao Tse-tung

One human being in four is now Chinese; one need only recall this to realize the importance of trade relationships. In this last quarter of the twentieth century, we no longer have to face the attitude expressed in the often-quoted reply given by Chien Lung, Emperor, poet and painter, to the British Ambassador who went in 1793 to suggest establishing trade agreements: 'Overpriced curios are of no interest to me. As you can see for yourself, we have everything we need; I can see no value in foreign or ingeniously designed objects, and I have no need for what your country may produce.'

China today, after twenty years of its new regime, has a stable government and, consequently, a continuity in its ideas. Commercial activities can therefore develop normally. Besides, the eventful twenty-five years which followed the revolution of 1911 gave ample proof, if proof were needed, of the commercial genius of the Chinese: when the civil war closed one market, ambitious or astute Chinese would find other outlets. Though at present, despite its tremendous efforts to become a major industrial power, China is not yet in the vanguard, its economy has still undergone such changes that it cannot fail to have an ever stronger influence on foreign markets. And here Chinese pragmatism has free play. Though Peking may occasionally use trade for political advantage, it still remains that business advantage has the ultimate priority.

But the political situation inhibits the expansion of business relations with the West: foreign commerce – part of the socialist plan for industrializing China – can therefore only play a marginal role, simply filling in the gaps in the domestic scene, as is clear from the trade figures. There is little point in the refusal of the Chinese leaders to publish their official documents – indeed it is somewhat ridiculous, given that all their trading partners, Russia included, publish their import statistics. From these we can analyse fairly precisely the real scope of Peking's foreign trade, its exact nature, its geographical provenance, its characteristics, its intended and admitted purposes (even though they are meant to be secret), and both its successes and its limitations.

'Having Your Door-key in Your Own Pocket'

Obviously the coming to power of the Communists has meant a complete reshuffle in commercial relationships. Great Britain, the U.S.A., Germany and Japan, for instance, all traditionally did business in China. Though of old, Tsarist Russia was a large buyer of tea, Communist Russia, between the wars did only a tiny amount of trading with China.

Exports and Imports, 1937–8

Countries	Imports from (average for 1937–8 in percentages)	Exports to
Japan	24·8	31·7
U.S.A.	18·3	19·4
Hong Kong	2·4	26·7
Germany	13·9	8
Great Britain	9·8	8·5
Eastern Europe	1	0·4
Total	70·2	96·7

These figures are taken from the League of Nations International Trade Statistics for 1938.

At the end of the second world war, the Kuomintang received large quantities of foreign currency from the United States, but the corruption of Chiang Kai-chek and his generals and ministers, combined with inflation, led to a catastrophic deficit in the balance of payments: the gross price index rose in three years (September 1945–August 1948) from 100 to 1,368. Six months later, Chinese foreign trade had virtually ceased to exist. The establishment of the people's Republic, in October 1949, was followed by a complete overthrow of all the traditional commercial patterns and a total and stringent control by the State over all foreign trade and exchange. Liu Shao-chi, the second-in-command in the new regime, put forward Peking's attitude to foreign trade in these terms:

Imperialism has been driven out of China, and the imperialists' privileges have been abolished. Import taxes and foreign trade have become major means of protecting the development of our own national industry. In other words, China will keep its own door-key in its own pocket; no longer will that key be in the pockets of foreign imperialists and their lackeys, as it used to be. Chinese industry will, from now on, no longer suffer from the competition of the merchandise they used to sell us at artificially low prices. China's raw materials will henceforth be used first and foremost to satisfy the needs of our own industry. This will overcome the major obstacle that Chinese industrial expansion has had to face in the last hundred years.

Speech, 1 May 1950

The Korean war caused a delay in establishing new machinery for foreign trade, and it was not until 7 August 1952 that the Ministry for Foreign Trade was established – a ministry that was to be little affected by the enormous reform of the administration resulting from the new institutions set up by the Constitution of 20 September 1954. Foreign trade, thenceforth a state monopoly, still preserves almost intact the general pattern it had twenty years ago. Since the details are not important, I will simply point out that the volume of Chinese international business is fixed by yearly plans, which are themselves worked out on the basis and within the framework of the five-year plan in force at the time: thus the volume of exports and imports is fixed in advance for each year.

The planning of foreign trade is an integral part of the planning of the whole economy. An article in the leading Peking non-party daily, *Ta Kung Pao*, admits this frankly:

The chief job of our foreign trade is to assist the socialist industrialization of the country; it is to procure the industrial equipment and machinery we need. ... Since this is something necessary for our industrialization, then we must import; and since we must import, we must also export. . . . We should be very clear as to the importance of organizing our exports efficiently, and achieving the programmes established in our plans. . . . Exports are very closely related to the advance of industrialization in our country. . . . Our foreign trade bears a heavy responsibility in relation to the economic construction of the State, in the framework of the five-year plan. By trying to increase our exports, we are trying to speed up the industrialization of our country.

Ta Kung Pao, 14 June 1954

A List to One Side
Trade with Russia Before the War

Year	Exports	Imports
	(in percentages of the total)	
1935	0·9	0·7
1936	0·2	0·6
1937	0·7	0·6
1938	0·6	0·1

Though Russia's share in Chinese foreign trade before the Second World War was minimal, with the coming of the Communists to power things changed. The fundamental principles of Chinese foreign policy consisted in moving in one direction only. Mao stated this quite explicitly:

Forty years' experience with Sun Yat-sen and twenty-eight with the Chinese communist party have convinced me that to win and consolidate our victory we must opt for one side . . . The accumulated experience of those forty years and those twenty-eight years makes it clear that the Chinese must stand *either* on the side of imperialism, *or* on the side of socialism; to that rule there can be no exception. It is impossible to bestride the two: there is no third way. . . . On the international level, we belong to the anti-imperialist front led by the Soviet Union, and to receive the true help of our friends that is the side to which we must turn.

Democratic Dictatorship of the People

This policy was summed up by Po I-po, the Minister of Finance (purged in the Cultural Revolution) in the phrase: 'The Soviet Union of today will be the China of tomorrow'.* Russia, the first country to recognize the Peking regime, was to be far and away the most important trading partner of the new China. Huge-scale contracts were signed between Stalin and Mao in 1950, and Mao went to Moscow for the first time in his life, and actually spent three months there. Despite the 1951 embargo,† other agreements followed, in 1953, 1954, 1956, 1958, and 1959. Even after Stalin's death, these agreements continued to manifest Russia's desire to help people's China become industrialized. Obviously Russia did not give such aid from mere kindness of heart: it received a commensurate return. The credits granted by Moscow were indeed relatively modest, which was only natural, since Russia had also to contribute to the industrialization of the European socialist countries, and was herself expanding rapidly on the industrial front. However, the aid she gave was certainly considerably less than the Kremlin wanted the world to think. In fact, economic aid in the strict sense only represented 16·2 per cent of Russia's commitments in China. Far the largest part – 34·3 per cent – related to debts following the Korean war, of which the Kremlin demanded repayment in 1956–7 (while the 'eternal' friendship between the two countries was still in full force). In addition there were credits – 23·8 per cent – granted for 'buying back' Russia's shares in the four combined Sino–Soviet firms, and the military equipment of Port Arthur; and the other, unidentified expenses –

* From his report on the financial results of 1952, and the budget for 1953, 2 February 1953.

† The U.N. General Assembly adopted an American resolution on 18 May 1951, urging all member nations to impose an embargo on sending any products that might be of strategic value to Communist China, which was condemned as an 'aggressor' in Korea. But after the armistice had been signed in Korea on 27 July 1953, the movement to modify the restrictions in force on trade with Peking became more and more powerful. On 30 May 1957, Great Britain unilaterally declared a series of measures to relax the restrictions, a decision that was to be the prelude to a gradual lifting of the embargo.

Soviet Loans to China (1950–57)

Form of loan	in millions of dollars	per cent
Economic loans	336	16·2
Credits allowed for the military installations of Port Arthur, and the transfer of the Soviet shares in the four combined firms* to China	535·3	23·8
Debts incurred during the Korean War	771·5	34·3
Unidentified aid	579·2	25·7
Total	2,252·0	100·0

* Sovkimetal (Sinkiang Company for rare non-ferrous metals)
Sovkineft (Petroleum Company of Sinkiang)
Skoga (Society of Civil Aviation)
Sovkitsoudstroi (Company of Port Arthur Shipyards)

These figures are to be found in *The Chinese Mainland Review*, 1 June 1965, 'Soviet Loans and Repayment', by Ronald Hsia.

25·7 per cent – seem to be connected with military aid. It is important, however, to remember that the Kremlin did not impose the same principles on its dealings with Peking as on those with the countries of eastern Europe: even Professor W. W. Rostow, an opponent of Communism, admitted that 'Russia, in its trade with China, never made any attempt to exploit Peking.' (*Prospects for Communist China.*) Alongside its dealing with Russia, Peking also formed close commercial relationships with all the other socialist countries. And the importance of the part those countries played in China's industrial development has been acknowledged by the Peking authorities themselves. Effectively, Peking got everything the West refused to give it from Russia and the people's democracies who did not observe the 1951 embargo. Raw materials and machinery came to China from the East, though they could have come from the West; it certainly seems that some came rather a long way round. Hence, the part played by Russia and the socialist countries in Peking's foreign trade was bound to increase.

Exports to and Imports from Russia, 1957–68

in millions of roubles (1 rouble = 50p)	1957	1960	1962	1965	1966	1967
Exports	973	1,182	799	634	578	504
Imports	792	1,141	431	474	494	360
Total	1,765	2,323	1,230	1,108	1,072	864

These figures are to be found in *Kommunist*, No. 12, Moscow, August 1968, pp. 102–12.

During the first ten years of the regime, therefore, trade with Russia and the Communist bloc represented two-thirds of China's foreign business, the maximum of 78 per cent being reached in 1954, and the minimum of 63 per cent in 1958.

The disagreements between the two Communist giants – which there is no room to analyse here – were to be the prelude to a striking diminution in these interchanges, but not a complete cessation. In fact, since 1965, there even seems to have been a certain improvement in Sino-Soviet commercial relations: on 29 April, a trading agreement was signed, to be completed in July and September respectively by a further agreement, and a contract to provide aeroplanes, helicopters and sundry other things. In addition to this, it must be remembered that Rumania, which cultivated China's friendship, and had never broken off business relations with Peking, was able to buy from Russia anything it could not itself produce.

A Blow to the West

When its interests are at stake, the Kremlin is not troubled by scruples. What happened in Hungary in October 1956 and in Czechoslovakia in August 1968 proves that the Soviets do not stop to quibble over means. The same thing happened to Peking in July 1960, when the Russians withdrew their experts and cancelled all their contracts. The Peking official daily complained bitterly:

... The Soviet authorities are extending the ideological differences between the Chinese and Soviet Communist parties into the sphere of the relationship between the two States, by deciding unilaterally, and without warning, to recall all the Soviet experts who have been helping us in our labours up to now – a total of 1,390 – and furthermore, tearing up 343 contracts and supplementary contracts for experts, cancelling 257 plans for scientific and technological collaboration. Since then, they have also considerably reduced the provision of complete plants, and of parts which are of major importance to our industrial equipment.

Renmin Ribao, 4 December 1964

Possibly because they felt the danger of building up on their own frontiers the power of a vast China which might one day be tempted to recover disputed territory, the Soviets, by their unilateral decision, had certainly delivered a crushing blow to the Chinese. Peking was made sharply aware of the vulnerability of having an economic system based on close and exclusive collaboration with one other country: transport was hampered by lack of fuel, factories remained unfinished, plants could not be used for lack of technicians or spare parts. ... The tensions created by the Great Leap Forward – which was, as we have seen, out of all proportion to the country's possibilities – aggravated by poor harvests and the withdrawal of Russian aid (and remember that for Peking it was only these last two factors that could possibly explain the failure of the Great Leap) almost turned the whole economy upside down. The Chinese responded with energy and realistically: and this was the real blow to the West. Though much has been written about the earliest efforts by Europeans to form links with China, little has been said about China's own efforts, long before the Christian era, to expand its trade westwards, before direct commercial relations were established with the Portuguese in 1516, followed by the Spanish, the Dutch, eventually the English, and last of all, the clipper fleet which brought the American flag into Chinese waters. Unfortunately, given the instability of its society, the endless internal troubles, the civil war, and continual breakdown of transport arrangements, China was unable to profit from all the advantages of having a world market available.

The new relationship with the West now forced upon China (apart of course from the U.S., for any country needs one mortal enemy to keep people on their toes) made it possible for Peking to keep its level of exports to Moscow high enough to repay its debt to Russia by the beginning of 1965. (Declaration of Li Che-jen, 10 January 1966).

With the support of other socialist countries, China was able among other things to establish aeronautical firms, an industry for atomic energy, factories producing modern locomotives and heavy machinery, power stations, and installations for the production of special forms of steel and industries using nonferrous metals. Imports were given absolute priority (35–45 per cent of the total) together with means of production and transport. Then came light industry, then raw materials other than food (10–15 per cent), chemical products (8 per cent) and finally, foodstuffs (4 per cent).

Alongside the review of the policy of industrialization, and the priority accorded to the production of food for home consumption, there was also a radical change in the order of priorities:

Change in Priorities, 1960–62

Sectors	1960	1961	1962
	(given in percentages)		
Manufactured products	27·7	16·6	15·0
Capital goods	38·4	21·3	15·6
Raw materials (not food)	15·0	14·1	19·6
Foodstuffs	4·0	32·0	35·0

The sudden progress of 1961 was to continue well beyond 1962: with most industrial plant being used for agriculture – factories producing fertilizer, for instance, or agricultural machinery. But this total change of priorities – with agriculture henceforth the basic sector and industry the dominant factor – contrary to Marxist–Leninist teaching, brought with it a complete reversal of the pattern of exchange, to the detriment of the other socialist countries. And the situation was made worse by the fact that since 1961, China had been importing cereals (wheat in particular) which its own agricultural troubles made it impossible to provide adequately, and which have always been the Achilles' heel of the other Communist countries. So Peking turned to Canada, and even more to Australia, a rich grain-producing country with a small population, which will certainly have to play an ever more important part in Asia in the future.

So the word came from the tenth plenum of the Central Committee of the Chinese Communist Party in 1962 for a return to nationalism, a counting only on oneself suggesting a certain longing for autarchy: the millennial dream of the Middle Empire. This call to self-sufficiency uttered today by people's China, to create socialism by means of one's own powers, is reflected in the share China's foreign trade (both imports and exports) has in world trade as a whole. In terms of percentage of world trade the curve has gone like this:

1955	1·43	1960	1·53
1956	1·49	1961	1·12
1957	1·35	1962	0·97
1958	1·76	1963	0·86
1959	1·84	1964	0·92

Thus, with a level of barely one per cent, people's China, though containing a quarter of the world's population, lives outside the major commercial streams of the world. And that is why, though one certainly cannot deny the unfavourable repercussions of the Cultural Revolution on the economy and on foreign trade, with production and transport disrupted, for instance (though it created far less confusion in the economy than the Great Leap Forward), it remains that that cannot be the only reason for the level being and remaining so very low. The reasons in fact are to be found in Peking's determination to conquer underdevelopment within a semi-autarchic system. It would seem that China, having reached a stage of technology in which it can in future produce nearly everything produced by foreign systems or processes, sees little further need to import. Thus, this determination on China's part to reduce the volume of foreign trade, or at least to prevent its expanding, represents not just a yielding to circumstances, but a definite structural intention.

Going back to its Traditional Partners

With the new turn Peking's foreign trade took after the break between China and Russia, the 'traditional great powers' started out again on the road to China. And once again Shanghai harbour saw merchant ships flying the flags of Great Britain, West Germany, Japan, and Italy – even some from Latin America. There is no point in considering the details of the trading patterns; we need only pinpoint the essentials.

Special mention must be made of Hong Kong, which played a very fundamental role. Though that 'scented port', its people Chinese, the sea around it Chinese, and yet itself a colony of the British Crown, is a living anachronism, it can obviously only remain so because of certain material advantages of which China is the chief beneficiary. It is only by Peking's decision that Hong Kong still exists – and the precariousness of its independence is high-lighted if one recalls that its drinking water is provided by Canton (67 million cubic metres a year, sold at a fantastic price by Peking). Hong Kong depends on the will of God and people's China for its water supply, then, but also for its food; $2\frac{1}{2}$ million dollars worth of foodstuffs are bought from Peking each year.

Thus, though Hong Kong has provided a base for penetrating into China, ever since it was built in 1841, the situation is now the other way round, for this 'imperialist pimple' is now used by Peking as a trading-post for supplying the free world with food, consumer goods, and even some capital equipment marked 'made in China'. Western bankers and businessmen (especially Englishmen and Germans) were not slow to take note of the possible profits to be gained there. Even the Americans, despite their political attitude, have today got some 300 firms dealing with China as against only 80 ten years ago: thus enabling the Soviet press to denounce the 'Sino–American collusion' which, they affirm, takes place in the offices of Hong Kong. Business which fosters this kind of 'coexistence' brings enormous profits to Peking: Hong Kong buys from China goods averaging over the years a value of some 250 million dollars, whereas what it sells to China amounts to no more than 5 or 6 million. Ultimately the business sense – or pragmatism – of the Peking Government brings far more benefits (a strong foreign exchange in sterling and dollars) than disadvantages. Even the ideological inflexibility of the Cultural Revolution has had to yield to these 'compelling' arguments.

Trade with non-Communist Countries

(Figures are in millions of dollars)

Country	Chinese imports		Chinese exports		Total trade		Balance
	1967	1966	1967	1966	1967	1966	1967/6
Hong Kong	5·5	7·5	253	237·7	258·5	245·2	+ 13·3
West Germany	122	66	44	51	166	117	+ 49
Great Britain	76·5	46·4	51·4	58·8	127·9	105·2	+ 22·7
Australia	147·7	43·7	29·4	12·3	177·1	56	+121·1
Italy	44·6	24·2	29·8	24·5	74·4	48·7	+ 25·7
Canada	55·2	48·3	10·2	8·4	65·4	56·7	+ 8·7
France	35·4	34·8	22	24	57·4	58·8	− 1·4

Great Britain, which dominated world trade (both in merchandise and shipping) in the nineteenth and early twentieth century, had large economic interests in China. To save them – as also the future of Hong Kong – the British Government, with the unanimous approval of all the political parties and of the City, hastened to recognize the new regime in China as soon as possible. However, not until after the 1954 meeting in Geneva between Anthony Eden and Chou En-lai was there a clear improvement in the relations between the two countries. The upheavals of the Cultural Revolution in Peking, and the war of nerves in Hong Kong barely stirred the traditional British phlegm, and Anglo-Chinese commerce has continued to expand. Though, at first sight, Chinese trade may seem tiny in proportion to the whole volume of England's foreign trade, we must not forget that there is, in addition to direct transactions, a quantity of indirect business going via Hong Kong; unfortunately the statistics from Hong Kong give no detail as to the origin of the merchandise transferred, so it is almost impossible to gauge the extent of the Anglo-Chinese dealings which take place by that means. Though West Germany has not recognized their government, the Peking authorities have not forgotten that in the past Germany was one of their chief trading partners.

Trade with Germany before the War

(Figures are in percentages)

Years	Exports to China	Imports from China
1935	11·3	5
1936	15·9	5·6
1937	15·3	8·6
1938	12·6	7·4

Both sides want to re-establish the links. Bonn's refusal to have diplomatic relations with Formosa was favourably received in Peking. In addition, the contacts made with the West German consulate in Hong Kong were eventually to result, in the spring of 1964, in secret high-level discussions in Berne, with Minister Franz Krapf as the German representative. Back in Bonn, the then Minister of Foreign Affairs, Gerhard Shröder, declared himself strongly in favour of an agreement with Peking, but Washington still opposed it. Despite that, West Germany, the leading industrial nation of Europe, and object of the unconcealed hostility of Russia and the morbid jealousy of France, is also the main trading partner of Peking (see Table opposite).

Krupp, Demag, Friedrich Uhde, Henschel and Lurgi in particular, have agents in people's China; and the total value of German-Chinese trade has increased by up to 50 million dollars in one year! This sudden entry of Germany into the Chinese market, together with Peking's clearly announced intention of extending its dealings with Bonn, has been ill-received in Japan. But while relations between Peking and Bonn have improved, the gulf between East Germany and people's China has widened.

In fact the official Communist paper, *Neues Deutschland*, now considers it necessary to attack Peking, and to voice more and sharper criticisms. West Germany is the major beneficiary of Chinese imports: in 1968, the total trade between the two countries increased by a telling 22 per cent.

Italy, confronted with Germany's assault on the Chinese market, transformed by its own 'economic miracle', and thus in a powerful position, could hardly be content to sit back and watch. So Italian business firms have also made use of the commercial services of the consulate-general in Hong Kong, and of their trade office in Peking, to launch a vigorous campaign. Nor have their efforts been in vain, since Montecatini, E.N.I. and its offshoots, especially Snam Projetti and Agip, have all seen their order-books filled up for equipping whole factories (especially these producing fertilizer) and oil refineries. Trade between Italy and China has thus increased by over 25 million dollars in a year, making Italy sixth on the list of Peking's non-Communist suppliers. Australia has first place because, by buying wheat from there, people's China can sell more rice and thus earn foreign exchange. For, while rice is sold at 120 dollars a ton, imported wheat only costs 70, and the profit Peking gains from this makes it possible to buy industrial equipment abroad. Then too, since the vast mass of the people in China is concentrated in coastal areas which cannot produce enough food for them, imports of Australian wheat are also a means of freeing the still over-burdened rail communications with the interior to carry equipment, raw materials and workers. There is the further advantage that more rice can be grown per hectare than any other cereal crop.

Peking is also anxious to establish reserves, first in order to be protected against the recurrence of such difficult situations as arose in 1961–2, but also against the possibility of future disputes which might stop foreign supplies coming into the country. While Sino-Australian relations thus increase the potential of China, they are received with equal favour in Australia, which is already finding some difficulty in selling its produce in Western Europe and elsewhere, and therefore finds it advisable to preserve as many business contacts as possible with Peking.

Agricultural Production Compared

	Yield in quintals per hectare (1 quintal = 100 kilos)				
	Cereals other than rice	Potatoes	Rice	Number of hectares per tractor	Artificial fertilizers used (in kilos per hectare)
China	8·10	70	25	1,300	6 to 7
U.S.S.R.	8·60	93		190	10·5
U.S.A	14·10	211		40	39·6
Western Europe	25·70	188		21	138·8

The Cultural Revolution and Foreign Trade

There is certainly no doubt that Chinese planning is a far cry, in practice, from Marxist theory. And when it comes to foreign trade, the divergence is obvious indeed, since that is something relatively independent of the general planning system. People's China, as I think has been made amply clear in the preceding chapter, is still, twenty years since the advent of the Communist regime, an underdeveloped country, despite having nuclear armaments; its needs are virtually limitless due to the weakness of its infrastructure and the tremendous increase in its population. Peking therefore must, willy nilly, turn to foreign trade for help.

The third five-year plan (1966–70), having preserved the change in priorities decided after the semi-failure of the Great Leap Forward (agriculture now being the base sector, and industry the dominant factor), the need to import is more obvious than ever. (Though here again, we must not expect more than an increase of 5 to 10 per cent because of the relatively marginal nature of China's foreign trade.) But any increase in imports must depend on an improvement in production at home (with diversification, improved quality, and increased quantity): there must be more exporting of farm produce, both animal and vegetable, and of textiles – for Peking, for obvious political reasons, refuses to sell the strategic products of its sub-

soil, like wolfram, cobalt, manganese and so on. Yet, in the
context of the present five-year plan, China's foreign trade
depends on its exports of textiles and farm produce, but also on
what middle-term (i.e. three- to five-year) credits it can obtain –
at present its credits extend for no more than eighteen months:
this will be no problem, for Peking, which always stands by its
commitments, considers it vital to honour them when they fall
due. The economic recovery begun in 1964 – except in the
unlikely event of there being a repetition of the Great Leap
Forward – will continue with a growth rate of 9 per cent for
industry, 2·5 per cent for agriculture, and a gross domestic
product of 6 per cent. The indirect and cumulative effects on the
political and administrative level, flowing from the cultural
revolution – especially between May 1966 and March 1967 –
did not have too serious an effect on foreign trade. Though
China had less to sell in 1967 than in 1966, this was not because
of a drop in production, which, as we saw in the previous
chapter, was far less affected than many people in the West
believed, but was due far more to problems in internal transport
(disturbances of rail traffic) and in the chartering of ships.

The renewal begun in 1962 led to a rise which continued up to
1966, when the record of 1959 was repeated (see graph). Obviously
the Chinese leaders are well aware of the importance of exports
(and at times they have followed an extraordinarily bold policy

Exports and Imports, 1959–67
(In thousands of millions of dollars)

	Exports	Imports	Total trade
1959	2·2	2·1	4·3
1962	1·5	1·2	2·7
1963	1·6	1·2	2·8
1964	1·7	1·5	3·2
1965	1·9	1·9	3·8
1966	2·2	2·1	4·3
1967	2	2·2	4·2

Foreign Trade in the People's Republic of China (1952–67)
(imports + exports)

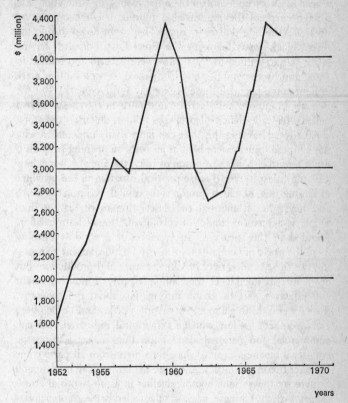

of dumping*) since it is only by selling more than they buy –
and in 1967 they bought 6·5 per cent more than in 1966 – that
they can make the profit that will enable them to accumulate

---

* In Iraq, for instance, Peking sells at prices 20 per cent lower than the
Japanese rates, which are already 30 per cent below those of Western nations.
In Tunisia, Peking sells 10 per cent below the Japanese, and 40 per cent
below the French price. In Ceylon, Peking provides rice at 3 dollars a ton
below the market price. All good anti-imperialist practices!

currency reserves; helpful too are the funds sent home by the Chinese abroad which will vary between 50 and 100 million dollars a year. By a careful control over the money in circulation and foreign currency, Peking was able to bring its currency reserves up to 645 million dollars in 1957. They went down during the three 'black' years following the Great Leap Forward; having fallen to 320 million in 1962, they were back to 400 million in 1964, and by the end of 1965 had passed the 500 million mark (a figure on a par with those of Norway and Denmark). But the increase in imports and decrease in exports in 1967 resulted in a balance-of-trade deficit of over 250 million dollars – the worst since 1955. Knowing this, one can more easily understand why the Chinese leaders were bent at all costs on opening (though it was a month late, in the autumn of 1967) the fair of Kwangchow (Canton), despite a still tense political situation in the province of Kwangtung, of which Canton is the capital. 'Canton the Red', and never has it merited the description more than it does today, is a historic citadel of revolution. Its semi-annual fair, founded in the spring of 1957, makes it a window opening on to the world of China. It is primarily a national event, expressing the riches and variety of Chinese work and production, but at the international level, the Canton fair plays a most important and effective part in giving information about the economy. Twice a year, lasting a month (15 April–15 May and 15 October–15 November), the fair, which is agricultural, industrial, regional, commercial and national all at once, thus makes Canton the country's business capital, since foreigners from all parts come together there, and meet in the huge Exhibition Hall in Haitchou Square by the various booths, dealing in a most cordial atmosphere with the Chinese, who are unequalled in the art of negotiating simultaneously with competing sellers.

The first fair (March–April 1957) showed 12,000 items in an area of 9,000 square metres, and welcomed 1,200 visitors from twenty different countries; ten years later there were 20,000 products displayed in an area of 47,000 square metres, 7,800 visitors from sixty countries and five continents, and a volume of business (both export and import) twenty times greater than at the first fair. It must be noted that the agents of firms from

Japan, and some countries in western Europe, who were showing in Canton, would often sell their samples and models on the spot at low prices (thus avoiding having to take them home, and saving considerable transport costs) in the hope of getting orders for them. Without complete figures for 1969 – having only those for the first three months, I think it would be risky to estimate from them for the whole year – I shall merely point out that it seems clear from the developments of the last three years that any economy, whether Communist or not, absolutely needs some degree of stability.

Japan: China's Natural Associate

As Peking celebrated twenty years of Communist rule, trade between China and Japan was still far from its pre-war level, when the Japanese empire sold almost a quarter of its total exports to China; but it was already well above the rate of Japanese trade with Europe. For reasons of history (age-old links of dependence or subjection), of geography (the closeness of the two countries which makes transport so much cheaper), of economy (the complementarity of the two economies at their present different stages of development), trade between the two countries, which has been continually expanding for some years now, will expand even more for reasons both financial and strategic. Financial, first, since the rising rates of interest everywhere makes it essential to pay in one's own currency rather than foreign exchange, if one's economy is not to be weakened by a draining of the country's capital; hence Japan stands to profit greatly by financing its business by trading in kind. Strategic also, because the need for a supply of raw materials demands that the sources of supply be diversified. Now, the new Japan, which started from scratch twenty-four years ago, is already almost level with Russia and expects to overtake it during the course of the next ten years; it will therefore soon find itself in the centre of the confrontation between China and the U.S.A. As an Asian power, Japan could hardly avoid trading with Peking: its own economic balance demands it. As a Western power, a member of the O.E.C.D. (Organization for Economic Coopera-

Pre-war Trade with Japan
(in percentages)

	Exports	Imports
1935	15·6	14·7
1936	16·6	15·1
1937	16·1	10·4
1938	23·7	15·3

These figures are to be found in the *League of Nations Annual Statistics for International Trade*.

tion and Development), Japan cannot break through the safety barrier established by America round the Communist countries of Asia without imperilling its trade with the U.S. This position is all the more uncomfortable in that the two opposing powers have formidable weapons: the Americans can threaten to discontinue all orders; the Chinese can threaten to cut off supplies and close markets, thus imperilling the whole balance of the economy. The prudence with which Japan is trying to feel its way between the United States and China proves how well aware it is of the tiny margin for initiative left to it amid these contradictory demands.

Thus, despite the absence of diplomatic relations, Tokyo and Peking have worked out a *modus vivendi* in their business dealings: they have the formulae of 'friendly firms' and the 'L-T Agreement'. It was on 1 June 1952 that the first unofficial agreement was signed between the Chinese Committee for the Development of International Commerce and certain special Japanese organizations founded to foster business with people's China ('friendly firms' meant firms approved by the Chinese Communist Party). After that there was a steady increase in dealings between Peking and the 'friendly firms' in Japan: 34 million dollars in 1953, 151 million in 1956. In 1956 alone, 108 Japanese delegations visited various parts of China, as against 106 during the whole period from 1949 to 1955. But Japan's dealings with South Korea inevitably enraged Peking, which responded by a cut-back in trade relations. Thus Sino-Japanese dealings fell to 23 million dollars in 1959 and 1960; however, the withdrawal of Soviet aid forced Peking to turn to Japan, and since then trade between the two countries has again increased enormously: 47 million dollars in 1961, 84 million in 1962, and 420 million in 1966. By then there were some 350 'friendly firms', with forty of them combining to keep 90 permanent representatives in China. It is important to note that some of them are simply off-shoots of far larger firms, but because of their business connections with the U.S.A. (and even Formosa!t their true identity has to be concealed. (This is similar to the situation in France, where, since the Government imposed import quotas to prevent the market being flooded with Japanese products, French importers have taken to buying a lot of Japanese goods anonymously in federal Germany, thus withholding from the French customs the duty they would normally have had to pay.)

These dealings between China and Japan were effected on the basis of the pound sterling. But when France launched her superhuman attempt to bring down the dollar, and with it all other currencies too, Peking realized that France's financial and monetary offensive against the U.S.A. was pushing the imperialist world towards a further break-up (*Renmin Ribao*, 3 April 1968). And since it wanted by some means both to hasten that break-up and make Paris suffer for the 'imperialism' it so continually attacked, Peking hurried to get rid of its French francs. American banks (Chase Manhattan Bank, First National City Bank, Bank of America) bought all the francs offered by the banks in Hong Kong, and sent them to New York where they were officially changed. In so doing, the American banks spared the already weak French franc any additional damage just on the eve of the terrific upheavals of May–June 1968. Banking circles in China and Japan considered after that that the French franc was subject to too much fluctuation, and it was therefore decided in June 1968 to use the Japanese yen as the basis for their business dealings. Finally, on 21 November 1968, Peking decided to accept no more French francs or pounds sterling. China, with its strict control of all external finances, continued to accumulate gold reserves – in fact in the early months of 1968, she bought another thirty tons of gold in London. (Japan and Russia, who continued to do their business in dollars, did, none the less, in their commercial contracts, use the Swiss franc to back up their promises.)

During the year 1962, following first unofficial and then official talks, an agreement was made between the Japanese liberal democrat ex-minister, Tatsunosuka Takasaki and the Chinese minister Liao Cheng-chi, President of the Sino-Japanese Friendship Association. This document, signed on 9 November 1962 for a five-year period by both men, was to become generally known as the 'L-T Agreement'. The volume of commercial operations which took place under the terms of the L-T Agreement in its first five years developed as follows:

> 1963 – 64·3 million dollars
> 1964 – 114·4 million dollars
> 1965 – 182·8 million dollars
> 1966 – 200 million dollars
> 1967 – 190 million dollars

Note, however, that the trade between the two countries increased more rapidly under the aegis of the 'friendly firms' than that of the L-T Agreement. Nineteen sixty-seven was the end of its five years; now during that summer, the Japanese Prime Minister, Eisaku Sato, made an official visit to Peking's enemy number one, Generalissimo Chiang Kai-chek, the 'recluse' of Formosa (which had become Japanese territory following the war of 1894–5, and remained so up until 1945). Having denounced the Prime Minister as the 'reactionary accomplice of imperialism', and expelled from China twenty of the ninety permanent representatives of Japanese firms there, Peking refused to resume the L-T Agreement for a five-year term, but only accepted it for a year, limiting the volume of business to 110 million dollars in each direction. China intended in this way to make it clear that she knew what strong pressures were being put on the liberal Democratic Party, now in power for over twenty years. A new group came into being inside the Japanese Parliament in April 1968, men determined to assist in restoring normal relations with Peking. The Chinese leaders felt confident that the Paris Conference on Vietnam must eventually result in an armistice, thus putting a stop to American arms orders – 750 million dollars' worth in 1967 alone – and that Japan would have to make up for this by increasing her exports to China. Furthermore, if the new President of the United States, Richard Nixon, were to yield to the pressures of the protectionists, the Japanese economy would suffer a blow whose effects could be immeasurable (indeed, it was only thanks to President Johnson's determination that the United States customs had during his term of office established no barriers to protect the economy from the influx of Japanese products, especially steel). Yes, the Chinese were well aware what cards they held, and they played them with consummate skill. Keeping back their two major trumps – West Germany and Italy – Peking insisted that henceforth Tokyo must give proof of its good intentions – in other words, must recognize people's China, and break off relations with Formosa. It would be Utopian in the extreme for Japan to hope to increase her exports to China without having to make any concessions; yet a thaw would not be easy.

Could Tokyo shake itself sufficiently free of Washington to assume political and economic independence? Yet was it not already quite clear that there must inevitably develop a symbiosis between Japan and China (with Japan providing industrial and commercial dynamism, and China the manpower and raw materials), which would then make the Sino-Japanese bloc economic leader of three-fifths of mankind, a prime force to be reckoned with in the world?

The Aided Giving Aid

Peking's aid to the Third World is really outside the scope of this chapter, but must be given a mention here because that aid is part of the totality of Chinese foreign trade. Unique in both financial and technical organization, the aid given by China to the underdeveloped countries of the Third World is also unique psychologically. Peking has two major objectives: to oust the imperialists (and incidentally the U.S.S.R. also) from the positions they had previously held – in other words, to stop the

West seizing the wealth of the Third World, get rid of schools and all other cultural influences of the West, take over mines, oil wells, refineries and other industries established by Western firms – and have the 'Chinese way' accepted as a pattern for development. Mao once said, quoting Li Li-fam, a prime minister under the Tang, that he had honey in his mouth and a knife concealed in his bosom.* But today the Chinese leaders conceal nothing. Nor do the Soviets. Which is why the verbal abuse between Peking and Moscow, though it will never actually lead to fighting – should never blind us to the fact that there is unity in opposition to the West; thus in the Afro-Asian Conference in Cairo, the Azanian (South Africa) delegate made a violent attack on 'the U.S.A. which uses economic aid as a means to keep control of the economic development of the country receiving the aid'. This completely unambiguous statement expresses the desire shared by Moscow and Peking to drive the West out of the Third World (even though each of them may wish it for its own sole benefit). Then, as Mao has said: 'Imperialism will be destroyed in the world, which will become socialist.' (1 September 1963.)

It is through two-way trade with the underdeveloped countries that China best establishes herself. (From force of circumstance, 'ignored' as she is by the U.N., merely an observer in the Communist Common Market, Comecon, people's China is in no position to take part in any multilateral policy.)

So we find the Chinese offering loans at low rates of interest, or even none at all, but always well below the 2·5 per cent asked by the Russians. Furthermore, those loans are long-term ones (10 or 20 years) whose repayment need only begin ten years after they are granted; and this aspect of Peking's aid is greatly appreciated. Then too, while Moscow supports the setting up of industrial complexes giving priority to heavy industry, Peking, by contrast, plans enterprises far less demanding, calling for less investment, making use of the country's natural products (textiles, paper-mills, sugar refineries, cement-works, and the like), which give work to a local labour force and which, though they may require relatively larger numbers of workers, will also

* *Selected Works*, vol. III, p. 121.

produce quicker results – for instance produce that can be used or consumed at once. This system of small-scale enterprise represents to Peking a subtle means of enabling the new countries to get rid of products 'Made in France', or 'Made in Great Britain'. But Peking's supreme psychological skill appears in the stress it lays on the affinities linking all peoples who have in the past been colonized or semi-colonized, on the need for mutual trade arrangements, and above all, in presenting China in the guise of a country whose economic basis is agricultural, but which has managed both to advance its agriculture and become industrialized by combining modern technology with traditional methods. Thus Peking offers to underdeveloped countries the 'Chinese way' as a model which has been tested and found efficient. And, remember, it is a model that cannot fail to fascinate all non-white peoples.

Though China herself was desperately underdeveloped in 1953, and the aid she could offer then was small, it was to become considerably more extensive once the Twentieth Congress of the Soviet Communist Party determined to take an active part in the economic growth of the Third World countries. Once again, the Kremlin was revising its ideological postulates and tactical principles, for, since 1917, its policy had been directed to industrially developed countries; now, turning to the pre-industrial nations, Moscow was abandoning certain ideological principles: Lenin would never admit before 1917 that a revolution could succeed in Tsarist Russia, because the objective conditions for such a revolution were not present there; on the other hand, the Kaiser's Germany was considered the ideal ground for a revolution. (In fact, apart from Sultan Galiev in 1923, and later Mao Tse-tung, all Marxist theoreticians have held this theory.) Henceforth the Third World was to form a geo-political totality, since the communist objective is to unite all underdeveloped countries against the colonial system, the traditional support for the imperialist power of capitalism.

Up to the time of Russia's abandoning its aid to China in 1960, China, with the immense advantage of being a genuinely Asian country, had restricted its own aid to other Asian countries; but from then on, it extended it to all the new States in the world, especially those in Africa (new indeed, with seventeen military coups d'état in the course of six years among black African states!). To Africa it presented itself as an Islamic power, for after Pakistan and Indonesia, China is the third largest Moslem country in the world. Innumerable delegations (more than 5,000 Chinese in all) went from Peking to the Arab countries, where they would perform jobs well below the skills they were equipped for; with extreme prudence, these technicians would accept a salary barely higher than that of a trained manual worker in the aided country, and the austere life led by the Chinese there, even the diplomats, has made an enormous impression on Africans. Different indeed from the behaviour of any of the *Western* experts!

Peking has been clever enough to make the most of its aid to the Third World, being given credit for far more than its real value. The total aid given is something in the region of 2,132 million dollars, geographically divided thus:

Asia	1,411·7 million
Africa	303 million
Europe	211·2 million
Near East	146·2 million
Latin America	60 million

One thousand, two hundred and ninety-nine million has gone to Communist countries, and 833 million to non-Communist ones. But, despite its relative smallness, Peking's aid nevertheless represents a most effective means of penetrating the developing countries. There has not yet been enough time for this aid to have borne its full fruits, so it would be premature to try to pass judgement on it as yet. But this Chinese assault on the Third World is something which must profoundly modify the elements of the problem during coming years. It calls for no guesswork, to foresee that if the Chinese system of aid to the Third World achieves real success, Peking will have produced a model of development totally out of all proportion to the actual size of the aid given. But it is important that we remember also to look at the use people's China intends to make of the new materials it gets from the Third World, for if Peking uses them to increase its holdings of foreign currency in the world market, and if in doing so it manages to affect the balance of the world market in those raw materials, then the Chinese challenge to world commerce will be explosive in the extreme.

FOUR. THE MILITARY CHALLENGE

Power lies at the point of a gun.
Mao Tse-tung

The Chinese Communist Party, having been at war for most of its existence, having won power as a result of military operations, and describing even its peaceful activities in military terms, has always placed all its hope in its army. Mao was to spend twenty years, along with his colleagues, paying the closest attention and care to the business of military power, and turning his Communist troops into a loyal instrument for carrying out his domestic and foreign policies.

The People's Liberation Army, with its five million soldiers, sailors and airmen, supported by a semi-military militia comprising a reserve of some 200 million men, certainly represents a redoubtable force. It is the chief indication of the restoration and grandeur of China. It is, in addition, an element to be reckoned with in foreign policy, and a challenge to all the countries which have humiliated China in the past. The People's Army has thus become the instrument of the suspicious and fierce nationalism created by a century of occupation and economic exploitation of this proud and sensitive people by Westerners and the Japanese. The Chinese army today represents a force all the more formidable in that it assures a new mission far exceeding the narrow framework of its own territorial boundaries – a mission to destroy imperialism all over the world by means of universal revolution.

'. . . Like a Fish in Water'

Having grown out of the guerrilla warfare of the revolution, the Red Chinese Army, at the time of its foundation on 1 August 1927, was primitive but triumphant, and was known as the People's Army of Liberation; its victory complete, twenty years later, it was still revolutionary, and was to remain so up to the eve of the Korean war. That war clearly showed up the weaknesses of the People's Army, and resulted in two opposing schools of thought in Peking: as against those who wanted a professional army on the Soviet pattern (which, since it could not be established without Soviet help, implied a policy of close alliance with Moscow), there were those who supported modernization, though of a limited kind, taking it as read that the People's Army could not be disloyal to the methods, still less to the spirit of Mao, which made it the invincible body it was. Though only temporarily, it was the modernizers who won the day. On 20 September 1953, the Constitution of the People's Republic of China was promulgated; by its terms (art. 42) though the President, as Commander-in-chief of the armed forces, was responsible for national defence, though he appointed the ministers, could proclaim martial law, declare war, order mobilization (art. 40) and preside over the Committee for National Defence (a lofty body of some hundred members – marshals, generals and ministers – establishing a policy of war, or peace, or mobilization, and thus acting as the instrument for defining long-term military policy and strategy, though not controlling the general organization of the armed forces), he was not, in actual fact, ultimately in charge of national defence. All the armed forces of China were controlled by the Minister of Defence and the Chief of the General Staff, the second most important military leader.

The following week, General Peng Teh-huai, Commander of the Chinese 'volunteers' in Korea – successor to General Lin Piao who had, between 16 October 1950 and 15 January 1951, driven back the American forces under General MacArthur to almost a hundred kilometres beyond the 38th parallel – was appointed Vice-President in the Government, and Minister of National Defence. His admiration for the Soviets was total, and he at once set about putting into effect Soviet ideas: voluntary service was stopped and conscription established on 9 February 1955. Simultaneously there appeared a new military regulation which for the first time introduced ranks, stripes, decorations, advancement for efficiency, graduated pay. The People's Army abandoned the old austere garb and gait of the guerrillas in favour of uniforms and a style strikingly similar to the Soviet pattern. Indeed, in the autumn of that same year, the Chinese army even become endowed with a clutch of marshals wearing chestfuls of the most varied medals and decorations.* Thus there emerged a body of men with all the traditional qualities of officers, but also alas, the defects. The army, with the help of the increase in 'professionalism', quickly began to establish itself as a body apart, with the concomitant danger of isolation from the rest of the people.' The political commissars remaining in office did not see eye to eye with these new officers so proud of their privileges, and as the months went by, there was increasing friction between them and the malcontents from the former army. But all this struggle was concealed from the public with calculated obscurity. Marshal Chu Teh (who had become a Communist at Heidelberg) denounced in no uncertain terms the career-mindedness of these officers and their loftily scornful attitude to the politicians. Marshal Peng Teh-huai, who was strongly criticized before the military committee of the Central Party committee (a key body heading the thirteen military districts, and expressing the will of the Party to the generals in command of the regions, all of whom were members of the Party's Central Committee), did not favour his predecessor in Korea, Marshal Lin Piao, now appointed Vice-President of the Government, being made a member of the permanent committee of the supreme political office of the Party, and thus becoming one of the 'Top Seven' in the regime.

Khrushchev, flanked by his Minister of Defence, Marshal Malinowski, suddenly arrived in Peking on 31 July 1958. Nothing was known of the military problems discussed between the defence ministers of the two countries until, five years later, the Peking daily reported that the Kremlin had then made 'an

---

* It was on 23 September 1955 that the ten generals who were Vice-Presidents of the National Council for the Armed Forces were raised to the dignity of Marshals of China. The following are their names in (our) alphabetical order, and dates of birth: Chen Yi (1901), Chu Teh (1886), Ho Lung (1896), Hsu Hsiang-chien (1902), Lin Piao (1907), Liu Po-cheng (1892), Lo Jung-huan (1902, died 1963), Nieh Jung-chen (1899), Peng Teh-huai (1902) and Yeh Chien-ying (1897).

unjustifiable demand which would have placed China under its military control, and which the Chinese Government could only, legitimately and resolutely, reject'.* Khrushchev had barely declared – on 13 August in Smolensk – that there was 'apparently no possible thunder-cloud in the sky', when on 22 August Peking began its bombardment of Quemoy. Interestingly the Soviets made no comment of any kind for a week. The martial speeches of Eisenhower and Nixon put Khrushchev in something of a spot, since he had made a much-commented statement through Tass to the effect that 'The U.S.S.R. will come to China's aid should she be attacked by the U.S.A. . . . but as for the civil war which the people of China are waging against the Chiang Kai-chek group, we have no intention of being drawn into that.'† Peking then announced that the bombardment would be suspended on alternate days. The crisis of the straits of Formosa, which ended on 22 October 1958, as a result of the Soviets' 'cowardice,' did extremely ill service to Marshal Peng Teh-huai, and his days were thenceforth numbered. However, unaware that the ground was being drawn from under him, he added fuel to the fire of his enemies during the famous meeting of the Central Committee in Lushan from 2 to 16 August 1959 by making himself the spokesman for those who wanted to preserve the Sino-Soviet alliance. His defence of material advantage over moral brought him into open opposition with the Maoist conception of the revolutionary war. This was too much. Accused of the crime of 'right-wing opportunism', Marshal Peng Teh-huai was deposed by the Military-affairs Committee of the Central Committee, and no explanation was given of his dismissal. His fall also resulted in that of the Chief of the General Staff, the directors of the three major services (Politics, Education and the rear), and his two former Korean colleagues– his adjutant and his Chief-of-staff. But unlike similar situations in the U.S.S.R., there was no blood-bath.‡ The Marshal was

* *Renmin Ribao*, 6 September 1963.

† Communiqué of 5 October 1958.

‡ Following the purges of 1937–8, the Red Army was only a shadow of its former self. Thirteen generals of the army out of 15 went, 57 out of 85 corps-commanders, 110 out of 195 divisional commanders, 220 out of 406

dismissed, settled in comfort in a villa where he lived peacefully, though under close guard, and was finally arrested on 24 December 1966 in Chengtu (Szechwan province).

The consequence of this purge was that Marshal Peng Teh-huai, son of a peasant, thickset, full of vitality, whose face was honest and whose laugh was rich, who wanted armoured and mechanized divisions on the Russian pattern, and military manoeuvres rather than political ones, was succeeded by Marshal Lin Piao, son of an industrialist – thin, cold, dry, frail, the defeater of MacArthur and one of the greatest strategists in the war of movement, who had won his international reputation in the field, and simply wanted huge numbers of foot-soldiers recruited from among tough peasants filled with revolutionary fervour. Between the old and new ministers of defence there was a contrast in temperament, and a total opposition of ideas. With the coming of Lin Piao, of whom so little had been heard for seven years, the real rise of the army began. To the new Minister, since politics came first, the army must be politicized. And, on 30 September 1959, the day of Khrushchev's arrival in Peking, Marshal Lin Piao published a major military article outlining the development of the army – and the country – in the coming years: 'The army is a tool for the political battle. The troops must actively and spontaneously participate in the building up of the country, and in the movement of the masses.'

Starting in October 1960, the Marshal launched a movement intended to involve the whole of China: 'Study the thoughts of Mao Tse-tung.' Since politics was now to be the decisive thing, obviously the army's political department would be its most

---

brigadiers, all 11 vice-commissars for war, 75 out of 80 members of the Supreme Military Council, all but one of the general officers of the Navy. Ninety per cent of the entire body of those with general's rank, 80 per cent of the colonels, and 30,000 other officers, senior and junior, were killed: half of all the officers in the country. In 1939, there remained only 2 out of 5 marshals, the high command was left leaderless, the regional staffs, armies and army corps in total confusion: no war, however devastating, could have had so bloody a result.

important section. The regulations of July 1961 changed the relationship between Party and Army, strengthening the Party's control over it. From top to toe, a complete political hierarchy was created parallel to the military hierarchy and supervising it, with about 50,000 political commissars for the armed forces. Two years later, having shown their value, the methods in force in the army were to be extended to the whole country, with the slogan. 'Make the People's Army your model.' Following the reorganization that took place after the first session of the third National Assembly, and the re-election on 3 January 1965 of Liu Shao-chi as President of the Republic, Marshal Lin Piao became the first of the sixteen vice-presidents of the Government. National service in either army, navy or air force was lengthened by a year, and a group of officers put into key positions: a Marshal became President and a General Vice-President of the National Assembly, the six Vice-Presidents of the Council of Defence became Vice-Presidents of the Government; out of eight 'industrial' ministries, five were given to generals; Foreign Affairs to a marshal, Finance to a general; Atomic Energy to a marshal; Sport to a marshal; State Security to a general.

Mao 'thinks' that: 'In China, democracy is necessary not only to the people, but also to the armed forces',* so in May 1965 there was a radical democratization in that sector. To restore to the People's Army of Liberation the revolutionary quality it had in the heroic days of the Yenan Republic, Marshal Lin Piao, on 22 May, decreed the abolition of ranks – just as Trotsky did provisionally in 1917 in order to 'democratize' the Red Army. So, ten years later, the classless army that had existed before February 1955 was now restored. This abolition of ranks in China also threw into strong relief the snobbish and bourgeois nature of the Soviet marshals and generals, with all their gold braid and constellations of medals. And, further, within the country, it once again expressed China's uniqueness; in fact yet another slogan was coined to confirm the unity between people and armed forces: 'The army is in the nation like a fish in water.'

* *Military Writings*, p. 29.

To mark the twentieth anniversary of the Japanese capitulation signed on board the Missouri, the Peking daily (*Renmin Ribao*, 3 September 1965) published the famous long article by Marshal Lin Piao, 'Long Live the Victorious War of the People', which was in a sense a modern expression of the strategic principles Mao had worked out thirty years earlier during the civil war and the war against Japan. The people's war had defeated Japan: it would defeat the U.S.A.! There was certainly an intensification of political activity among the troops (in 1961 a third of all soldiers were Communists; by 1965, two-thirds), and this was to be extended to the nation as a whole. On 2 July 1966, every newspaper in China published an 'Open Letter' dated 11 March, in which Marshal Lin Piao urged 'the 700 million Chinese to make the thoughts of Mao Tse-tung fully their own'. The eighteenth of August 1966 marked the apotheosis: in front of a million Red Guards, Marshal Lin Piao, Minister of Defence and Chief of the Armed Forces, was presented by Mao to the people, acclaimed with him as his 'close comrade in arms' (an expression thenceforth adopted as official), and obviously designated to be his successor. Thus, since Lin Piao's appearance on the scene, the armed forces had finally become more important than the Party which had produced them. It would be impossible in future to separate the two for, thanks to the Cultural Revolution, Party and army have in a sense become one and the same thing.

Organization, Structures, Equipment and Capacity of the Armed Forces

The six military zones (North-east, North-west, Northern China, Southern China, South-west, and Eastern China) into which China had been divided after the Communists' victory were dissolved in September 1954.

National defence is today organized in thirteen military areas, three of which (Inner Mongolia, Sinkiang and Tibet) have a special status of their own; they are divided into military conscription areas co-extensive with the administrative units. Air space follows the same lines of demarcation. And lastly, since the changes made in 1960, the shoreline is now divided into three 'maritime districts': Whampoa-Canton (the Southern sea), Shanghai (Eastern sea) and Tsingtao (Northern sea).

Deployment of the People's Liberation Army

Military region headquarters	Provinces controlled
Canton	Hunan Kwangsi Kwantung
Shenyang	Heilungkiang Kirin Liaoning
Foochow	Fukien Kwangsi
Huhehot	Inner Mongolia
Kunming	Kweichow Yunnan
Lanchow	Shensi Kansu Ninghsia Tsinghai
Lhasa	Tibet
Nanking	Anhwei Kiangsu Chekiang
Urumchi	Sinkiang
Peking	Shansi Hopeh
Chengtu	Szechwan
Tsinan	Shantung
Wuhan	Honan Hupeh

Since conscription could provide 5–6 million recruits a year, the selection of the 8 or 9 hundred thousand boys to be called up at eighteen could afford to be extremely strict as regards their physical fitness and the nation's economic requirements, and also, indeed supremely, in the matter of political education. Since, too, active service was increased by a year in January 1965, thus making infantry service four years, service in the air force and other ground forces, as well as State Security units, five years, and naval service six years, the regime possesses a tool that is unusually homogeneous in its doctrinal fidelity.

Ground Forces

Obviously the army proper is far and away the most sizable of the forces, consisting in peace time of some 5 million men – almost as many as in Russia for a population three times the size – 90 per cent of whom are in the infantry, thus leaving a small proportion of specialists (artillery, engineers, tanks, communications, etc.).

This ground force is made up of 40 armies, each with 200 divisions, but all, for the moment at least, handicapped by the lack of adequate equipment. As in other armies, there are general reserve units, and 100 division-sized units not broken up into separate divisions (artillery, armoured, parachute, cavalry), and some 80 regiments in charge of weapons and other supplies. Administratively speaking, the Chinese People's Army has introduced no innovations; it is as dependent on the traditional forces of support as any other modern army: three soldiers are needed to supply for the upkeep of every four men in training. With their highly standardized basic armaments (all old-fashioned and diverse weapons having been handed on to the militia) the ground forces are also supplied with anti-aircraft rockets (of the Soviet type SAM-2), such as were used to bring down the American U-2 spy planes, whose wreckage is now on exhibition in the Military Museum in Peking. China has a firing ground for missiles which extends from Kiuchuan in Kansu Province to the Lop Nor desert in Sinkiang Province which is reserved for nuclear testing.

Though spending large sums to carry out programmes for developing nuclear arms and missiles, the Chinese also wish to equip and modernize their armed forces, and have set aside huge credits for supplying them with the highest-quality traditional weapons. It may help to make clear just how large they are if one realizes that five out of the eight ministries related to metallurgical work are devoted to military needs. Since the road network is still inadequate, the Chinese are not at the moment trying to develop heavy tanks on a large scale. The units allotted motored vehicles are still few in number, and fuel is still strictly rationed: indeed, since the falling-out between China and Russia, and the Kremlin's withdrawal of petroleum supplies, China has had to solve the further problem of finding supplies of fuel; it would take her fifteen years to create a petroleum industry that would make her completely independent. Though, objectively, the capabilities of her weapons industry are by no means negligible, they are still restricted both as to quality and quantity. China still produces only tiny quantities of heavy tanks, of artillery larger than 152 mm. or heavy engineering equipment.

On the other hand, the sparse network of railways in China is clearly not designed for military transport, with the result that bottlenecks arise which diminish their capacity still further. The army is therefore without a supply system geared either to its numbers or to the fact that it is spread out over the 10 million square kilometres of land. Thus, even were it called to fight on its own ground or in neighbouring territory, it could only have the poorest strategic mobility.

Sea Forces

Though considered exclusively as a land power because, for the present at least, her basic strength lies in her control of the continental land mass, China, with 12,000 kilometres of coastline has, in the past two decades, expanded her seafaring activities in a discreet but continuous fashion, both as regards her merchant and her naval fleets. The latter indeed has been the object of such attention as to develop steadily and most impressively: in 1949 it did not exist at all – its ships could not even get as far as Taiwan (Formosa); but since 1954, it has made such strides as to become the largest naval force in Asia. But with a total of 200,000 men available to the Chief-of-staff, the acting Admiral Hsiao Chiang-kuang, and his six adjutants and two political commissars, the navy looks rather small in comparison with the army and air force. The fighting fleet has the following sea-going vessels: 2 cruisers, 20 destroyers, 30 frigates, about 50 light torpedo boats, and 300 troopships; in addition it has some troop landing-craft. Destroyers and frigates are being built in large numbers in Shanghai and Canton. China is at present the only country, apart from Japan, with a long-term programme for naval ship-building. Since investment priority has been given to industry and agriculture, only modest funds are available for the purpose, and in addition, the expansion of the navy is also hampered by lack of trained personnel: since 1949, the only superior officers available to the navy have been former army officers, and it has been necessary to create a naval high command, and, in 1951, to found a people's Naval Academy, and two aeronautical schools.

The same is true in the submarine sector. There, too, quite evident lack of trained officers and crews has been the limiting factor, for up until the break with Moscow all the submarine officers were Russian. Now that enough Chinese have been trained, the navy has emerged from the period of stagnation in which it languished until 1960. Today the situation is a very different one, and in fact it is in its submarine fleet that the main strength of the Chinese navy resides. It has 40 of the W-type (whose range is up to 15,000 kilometres) and is building 3 more every year. It has an equal number of type-G missile-launching submarines (with a range of 30,000 kilometres, each armed with three missiles capable of taking nuclear warheads), thus presenting a major offensive power. China is at present directing her efforts towards producing missiles which can be launched from submarines. At the end of 1967, Peking tested some submarine rockets west of Port Arthur (prototypes built according to Soviet technicians' designs), each capable of carrying three atomic warheads.

Thus, therefore, despite having a certain power of attack, the Chinese naval forces remain at present essentially defensive; but their future could be virtually limitless, for the problems of the past now no longer exist. Then too, though her strength resides in her control of the continent, China no longer wishes to be solely a land power; and for that reason, the Chinese naval threat – a wholly new source of strength – now faces us with a fresh problem.

The Air Force

The air force, complementing the land forces, has about 3,000 modern planes, 2,000 of which are jets. There are a great many airfields (since there is a vast labour force to build them), which makes it easier to disperse the available planes, thus making them less vulnerable to attack.

This air fleet has developed very rapidly, for twenty years ago the Communist troops had not a single plane in their possession. The first large delivery from Russia (1,000 planes) took place during the Korean war. Today the Chinese air force has 50 squadrons of jet fighters – Mig-15, Mig-17 and Mig-19, all built now in China, as well as some Mig-21s, the last received from Russia – which can fly at mach 2, and carry two air-to-air missiles. To these have been added 20 squadrons of light bombers, twin-engined Il-28 jets, Tu-4s (the Russian equivalent of the American B-29s that carried the atomic bomb), a small group of long-range bombers, a squadron of helicopters, and a great many transport planes. China is certainly not building strategic bombers herself but, once into the nuclear phase, she may well by-pass that particular stage, just as she by-passed the plutonium stage in getting her H-bomb.

The air force, an elite corps under the command of General Wu Fa-hsien, with seven adjutants and two political commissars, is organized into nine groups, with some 500,000 men (navigation, ground and administrative staff), all subject to strict political control, and a considerable number of women pilots. There is even – though only for display purposes – one exclusively feminine fighter squadron. Though China today has the world's third largest air force, its real fighting power is not in proportion to the number of aircraft available to it. And there is one major handicap – temporary, perhaps, but particularly acute – and that is her backwardness in aeronautical construction.

So, spread out from the Sea of Japan to the boundaries of India, the land, sea and air forces of the Chinese People's Army of Liberation are something the whole world must henceforth reckon with. The objectives declared by Mao on the eve of assuming power have now, twenty-two years later, been achieved: '... We shall have not only a powerful ground force, but also a powerful air force and a powerful navy ...'*

The Militia, the Army's Right Hand

In addition to this permanent armed force of some 5 million men, 3 million of them trained fighters, there is a considerable reserve to which all men belong up to the age of forty. The first reserve numbers all non-commissioned officers and men who have completed their active service. The second reserve numbers all who, for one reason or another, have not been in active service: this second reserve also incorporates women with special skills (such as doctors). Anyone may be called on for active service during his or her first five years in the reserve. In addition, the army also has an auxiliary reserve: the people's Militia. Having been overshadowed for some years, the Militia has become increasingly important since November 1964, when a national conference laid great stress on its political and military qualities. This people's Militia – whose origins date back to before the civil war, and which has always been a very large body – though not quite living up to the West's concept of a 'nation under arms', does curiously recall some of the things said by Lenin (*The Proletarian Militia*) and even by Marx himself (Elberfeld lecture).

From the point of view of strategy, there is absolute confidence in the inherent superiority of men over arms, and in Mao's statement that bombs of any kind are no more than paper tigers. But with its brigades of tens of millions of men and women, and its perhaps too rapid growth, the Militia has, as the Marxist

* Opening speech of the first plenary session 1949. Consultative Political Conference of the Chinese People, 21 September, 1949.

euphemism puts it, suffered from a 'certain degree of formalism': in other words, a large number of units were not 'pure' enough (politically, that is). Hence the need to form *base units* in contrast with the *ordinary units*. The former, an elite corps of some 20 million people, includes men from 16 to 32, and women from 18 to 25, who are politically reliable and familiar with the concept of revolutionary war. Both receive two months of basic infantry training (except for those dispensed from active service), and then continue with two hours of training a day, and one hour of political education. All this obviously contributes to the physical hardening-up of the elite militiamen, and to preparing them psychologically for combat conditions. Militarily speaking, these remain defensive measures. And it is clear from the directives given to the Militia that their function is to support the regular army in case of invasion or attack from the air. . . . As their political indoctrination advances, arms are gradually distributed to the men and women of the Militia. These base units, thus designed to provide assistance and relief for the regular army in case of fighting, form in peacetime a valuable support for the 'security forces' (the 500,000-strong secret police).

As for the ordinary units, they make up a vast body of men from 16 to 50 and women from 16 to 32, not quite up to the standard of the base units, but still hand-picked, who serve both as a production force and a fighting body. As Mao recommends, 'The whole Party must concentrate its attention on war, must learn the science of war, must be prepared for war.'* The ordinary Militia are not armed, but are chiefly trained in guerrilla tactics: their duty is to defend their communes, and to use guerrilla resistance methods should the enemy invade the area of the country where they live. In resistance of this kind, the Militia's role becomes of fundamental importance in supporting the activity of the troops: army and Militia between them can force a far better-equipped enemy to wear himself out in an unending battle. The example of Vietnam is a precedent no one contemplating invasion will forget. Thus the only standardized element in the organization of the two militias is their terminology:

* Problems of war and strategy, *Selected Works*, Vol. II.

they are divided up into divisions, regiments, battalions, companies, sections and platoons, the sizes of which are determined by the size of the production force to which each unit is attached.

But the actual military potential of these two militias as a fighting force is another matter. The vast mass of the Militia – the ordinary units – poorly trained and without weapons, must obviously include dissatisfied and therefore not wholly reliable elements. Furthermore, the official press leaves us in no doubt as to the fact that, except in time of war, the economic function of the Militia is of far greater importance than its military one. Work and military training are coordinated, but work comes first. In short, the speed with which the Militia has been formed seems mainly designed to bridge the gap between an army quite adequate for peacetime and the vast forces that would be needed in case of major conflict.

Twofold Mission: Defence and Construction

Though its regular army is formidable, the Peking Government also has, in the People's Army of Liberation, one of the most diversified armed forces in the world. It has a twofold mission to fulfil: defence and construction. Manual labour plays a great part in the life of both officers and enlisted men. Since 1959, all officers, regardless of rank, have had to serve one month in every year as private soldiers. In this way 150,000 officers – 150 of them generals – are forced to engage in this extremely unpopular service. Only sickness or physical incapacity can excuse anyone. There are a very few highly specialized men who manage to escape, but infantry officers have no such luck.

Superior officers and subalterns are also often sent in groups to one or another of the communes where they have to do productive manual work for a few days – a duty appreciated little more than that of the month spent annually in the ranks. Thus, for several weeks in every year, about half of the regular army is doing non-military work. Whole divisions, for instance, will help in putting up dams to prevent flooding. Others will help in building barrages, canals or roads. Though laying railways is primarily the duty of the army's engineers, whole regiments of infantry may be co-opted to help them.

Other units are used as pioneers, and sent to 'colonize' border areas which are sparsely populated, often by rebel citizens. The only absolutely certain method of avoiding trouble there is Sinization through repopulation. Animated cartoons, dance festivals, exotic costume displays, films – every possible means is used to show the young people of China that the greatest service they can render the revolution and their country is to emigrate to the far west.

Still other units – especially since April 1959 – have been sent into the people's communes, to help with the work and organization and, incidentally, to keep an eye on discipline. The army also produces the uniforms its soldiers wear, and runs its own farms where cereals are grown, and animals and fowls raised for food.

By a large-scale dispersal of the soldiers who come from all parts of this vast country, the army strengthens the cohesion of China, a cohesion already to some extent secured by the human wall of the Militia. In addition, and more importantly, the People's Army of Liberation serves as a police instrument by means of which Peking can put into effect its political theories and ideas. The intervention of the army in the Cultural Revolution provided the most spectacular demonstration of this.

The Cultural Revolution and its Vicissitudes

'The Party commands the gun, the gun must never be allowed to command the Party.' When he made this statement on 6 November 1938, Mao certainly had no idea that in thirty years' time it might once again become burningly relevant. It was in February 1966 that the army's political department was to recall so imperiously, in a now famous 'Instruction to the Army', that it was for the Party to command the gun and not the other way round. The Cultural Revolution, launched by Mao and his most dedicated supporters – among them Marshal Lin Piao – was dictated by the logic of the increasing radicalization of Maoist power which had been discernible since 1959. Mao had sensed among the educated a quite definite tendency to try to form the rising generation into their own mould; and this he was determined to oppose with all the force of a convinced revolutionary. He was determined to get rid of this danger, to reawaken zeal for the revolution, especially among the younger generation, and turn them into an army of proselytes to perpetuate his policies. It was a bold, perhaps too bold, attempt to find new ways of creating a Communist society adapted to the situation of Asian countries. It began on 9 May 1963 – the date given in Mao's article in *Renmin Ribao* (17 July 1966) – but from May 1963 until June 1966, it remained in its latent phase. Since it is quite impossible to give a full description here of all the events as I experienced them, I shall simply recall briefly the main points one must keep in mind to understand the situation as it is now.

The Latent Phase

Mao, whose life is a mass of 'contradictions', was only too well aware of the key cards he must hold if he were to win the Party's support in case of a confrontation between the army and the propaganda machine. He knew, and remembered keenly and bitterly, that by losing them both from 1931 to 1934, he had been almost without influence in the Soviet zone (Kiangsi and Fukien Provinces) even though he had in fact conquered it. Having long and closely planned and examined the movement which was to burst into China's political history as the Cultural Revolution (a more exact translation would be 'great revolution of civilization'), Mao chose from among the nine surviving marshals Lin Piao, because not only was he the most loyal ideologically, but he also had the greatest influence on the army – or more precisely, influence over the largest part of the army. When the Cultural Revolution began in May 1963, the army was anything but monolithic: the armies of the north-western provinces and of Shantung still responded to the prestige of Marshal Peng Teh-huai, deposed four years previously. However, altogether they represented no more than 20 per cent of the total. The armies of the south-west and of Szechwan, with

Marshal Liu Po-cheng, fourteenth in the supreme hierarchy, were so unreliable that the Marshal had to be dismissed at once, and the purge in those areas was worse than anywhere else. The fact was that Marshal Peng Teh-huai, Marshal Ho Long and the political commissar Liu Chih-chien, were all natives of Hunan province, while Marshal Liu Po-cheng and General Lo Jui-chin came from the neighbouring province of Szechwan. Consequently, Marshal Lin Piao was left with authority over the armies of the north-east, the military areas of Peking, Wuhan (Hankow) and Canton – something over 50 per cent of the total fighting force. This disunity which had grown up among the military leadership was fraught with consequences, for it had its logical repercussions among their subordinates: a phenomenon typical of pre-1949 Chinese tradition.

When, in May 1964, the Little Red Book which presented a distillation of Maoism appeared, it was first, and indeed solely, intended for the army. Put out by army presses for the army alone, the little book of quotations was to appear in a new edition, again for the army, in August 1965, this time with a preface by the army's political department. (The first edition of 1966 for the Red Guards, the civilians, and in fact the whole world, of which over a hundred million copies were printed, appeared with an introduction written by Marshal Lin Piao.) Being Communists, the Chinese continued to believe that ideas mattered more than laws, the foundation more than the superstructure, and that man could always find salvation in following the right doctrine.

Meanwhile, Liu Shao-chi's re-election as President of the Republic on 3 January 1965 for a further term of four years was the start of a process that was to divide the Communist leadership deeply. In people's China there is no opposition to the idea of socialism and its basic organization; any differences of opinion among those at the top, whether civil or military, relate to the general conception of, and practical methods for developing, socialist society. This was clear at the time of the 'Hundred Flowers' when, on 2 May 1956, Mao launched his famous battle-cry: 'Let a hundred flowers bloom, and a hundred schools compete!' It was clear too when the 'Great Leap Forward' was adopted on 29 August 1958 in Peitaihao, and set in motion

by the Wuhan resolution of 10 December 1958. The Cultural
Revolution was one more demonstration of this – nor was it to
be the last!* On 18 April 1966, the army daily printed a long
editorial entitled: 'Let us raise on high the red flag of the
thoughts of Mao Tse-tung, and take an active part in the great
socialist cultural revolution.' Three weeks later, on 9 May,
China exploded her third nuclear bomb.

In the West, however, Mao's disappearance from the Peking
scene was attributed to his state of health – though any such
rumour was belied by his Olympic performance in the Yang-tse
on 16 July 1966, when he swam fifteen kilometres in an hour
and five minutes, in company with Wang Jen-chung, First
Secretary of Hupeh Province, and Deputy Mayor of Canton.

So, from his 'exile' in Shanghai, and later Wuhan (1
November 1965 to 18 July 1966), with Marshal Lin Piao and a
small group of supporters, Mao set about reconquering Peking.
On Wednesday, 25 May 1966, a great revolutionary 'date' but a
peaceful one, a new period began in the history of China. The
Cultural Revolution entered its phase of rebellion (July 1966 to
January 1967). The notice stuck up that midday on the walls of
venerable Peking University – and we were later to learn from
the bi-monthly intellectual Party review, *Hongqi*, on 16
January 1967, that it was Mao himself who had put it there –
gave the signal for a popular mobilization the like of which has
never been seen in any socialist country, not even during the
days of the Nazis in Germany.

The Period of Rebellion

Though, as in 1931–43, Mao had been obliged after 10 December 1958 to give up the actuality of power by resigning as
President of the Republic (a resignation officially accepted on
28 April 1959), he had still remained President of the Party, and
it was as such that on 18 July he launched a solemn 'special

* The *People's Daily* of Peking announced it thus: The great Cultural
Revolution is only the first one; in the future, it will be necessary to start
afresh many times. . . . The problem of the victory or defeat of the revolution
can only be resolved over a long period of time.' (*Renmin Ribao*, 18 May 1967.)

appeal to all members and supporters of the Central Committee',
informing them that he was coming to Peking to take part in the
plenary meeting of that committee which could not, by statute,
open without his being there. That same day, in the capital, the
army entered upon the scene. Marshal Lin Piao had the Chief
of the General Staff, General Lo Jui-chin, dismissed, to be
replaced on 1 August 1966 by General Yang Cheng-wu. A
press-agency dispatch from Peking announced a year later that
General Lo Jui-chin was 'opposed to the nuclear programme
supported by President Mao, and wanted to stop the development of long-range missiles by diverting research work to
methods of production.'* The following month, an editorial in
the *People's Daily*, discussing disputes within the army, was to
blame General Lo Jui-chin 'for having abandoned the principle
that politics must come before technology, having set his face
against the Militia system and its links with the concept of the
people's war, and having maintained that nuclear weapons had
fundamentally changed the laws of military strategy'.† Of the
two men who had succeeded Marshal Peng Teh-huai in 1959,
Marshal Lin Piao the soldier, and General Lo Jui-chin the
politician, it was the soldier who kept his job – an anomaly
which explains quite a number of things!

During that same day, 18 July 1966, troops took up positions
all round the area, in order to stop the units from Shensi who
had been sent to the capital by orders of the deposed Chief of
the General Staff. Only quick action by Marshal Lin Piao, and
the new Chief of the General Staff, General Yang Cheng-wu,
prevented a civil war. Appalled, no doubt, by the consequences
of his decision, the Secretary-General of the Party, Teng Hsiao-
ping, did a brisk about-turn, and cancelled the forthcoming
plenary meeting of the Central Committee convoked by the
President of the Republic, Liu Shao-chi. From then onwards,
events moved rapidly. The Chief of the General Staff and the
Minister of Security, General Hsieh Fu-chi, speedily and firmly
took the situation in hand. On 28 July 1966, four military planes
brought Mao and the other members of the Central Committee

* *Hsinhua*, 28 August 1967.
† *Renmin Ribao*, 15 September 1967.

still faithful to him into Peking. The Central Committee, convoked by the President of the Republic in order to depose Mao (thinking that he could copy the precedent set by the Soviets in October 1964 which did so well for Brezhnev) finally opened a week late, due to Teng Hsiao-ping's volte-face, but under the presidency of Mao!

In session from 1 to 12 August, the eleventh plenum of the Central Committee marked a spectacular turning-point in the history of Chinese Communism. On 8 August it published the sixteen points of a charter for the Cultural Revolution, in the form of a 'Decision by the Central Committee of the Chinese Communist Party on the Great People's Cultural Revolution', a document extremely favourable to the army. Article 15, mainly devoted to it, said in so many words that: 'In the armed forces, the Cultural Revolution and the socialist education movement must be carried out in conformity with the instructions of the military commission of the Central Committee of the Party, and the General Political Department of the People's Army of Liberation.' So the armed forces became the only class in Chinese society to make its own Cultural Revolution without having to refer to the Party's Group for Cultural Revolution. This special treatment was enormously significant. As far as one can judge, its purpose was to win the army's support in any future developments. And it was no coincidence that the day after that Central Committee session, Marshal Lin Piao, Minister of Defence, who had always given the Party the total support of the army, made a rapid ascent within the supreme hierarchy: from sixth in rank, he became second, and he became also the one vice-President of the Party. Basically, he was the heir presumptive. His rise, strikingly enough, was simultaneous with the big American escalation in Vietnam (autumn 1965 to spring 1966). The faithful few of the Cultural Revolution were now in a higher position than either the President of the Republic or the Secretary-Genera of the Party. And now Mao was going to arouse a general renewal, not, as Stalin would have, by action from the top by the Party apparatus, but by a call to the young people in whose hands the future lay. And, on 18 August 1966, the Red Guards appeared on the scene. The role of youth in the

Chinese revolution was already something of a tradition: the 'New People's Study Society' inspired by Mao in Changsha around 1915 was, after all, made up of students. Renewal and continuity: these remain the two major characteristics of the present-day revolution.

Meanwhile, on 1 August, the *People's Daily* had reported that Mao was asking the masses 'to copy the army by transforming factories, people's communes, businesses, educational institutions, public services, and all State and Party bodies into great and genuinely revolutionary schools'. On 18 August, in the famous Tien An Men Square, Mao, wearing for the occasion the green cotton military uniform with its cap with the five-pointed red star, was solemnly presented by Lin Piao with a red armband inscribed in yellow characters, *Hong Wei Bin* (Red Guard). Organized and guided as it was by a very strong leadership which began by allowing considerable latitude to the Red Guards, and then drew certain sectors of the population into it in order to convince them that this was *their* movement, their revolution – the Cultural Revolution, during its period of rebellion, certainly gave the impression that China was wracked by chaos. Now chaos is one of Mao's strategic methods, indeed one of his chief weapons. His closest 'companion in arms' said the same thing quite explicitly: 'Do not be afraid of disorder, since it will make it possible to identify harmful elements.'*

From then on, the Army daily (*Jiefangjun Bao*) often departed from military subjects to make pronouncements on art, literature and music. A number of senior officers took strong exception to this, and some air-force spokesmen went so far as to express a fear that military training might suffer as a result of this almost exclusive concern with political indoctrination. On 28 November 1966, the number 1 company of the Peking opera and two other theatre companies in the city were actually incorporated into the army! And at the same time, Mao's present wife, Madame Chiang Ching, was made Councillor of the Cultural Revolution to the Army. This sudden appearance of the wife of the President – the Red Emperor – was surely reminiscent of old Chinese legends of the empress who rises up at the

* Speech by Marshal Lin Piao, 3 March 1967.

end of a dynasty. However it would be hard to find a better example to illustrate the difficulties. The over-enthusiasm of the Red Guards, whose proselytizing was at times more than imprudent, antagonized a number of the Party leaders. Though the army, protected from the Cultural Revolution, did not take over, it was waiting (with its own forces intact) for that revolution to demonstrate its inability to achieve its stated purposes. However, in 1967 the situation was to change. On 1 January, an editorial published in the Peking papers announced a new impetus in the Cultural Revolution – it was to be extended to factories and farms, without consideration of the possible consequences to the national economy. It was at this point that the so-called 'revolutionary rebel' groups appeared on the scene (the literal translation would be 'revolutionaries in revolt'). Again, it was renewal and continuity side by side; for in fact the myth of rebellion has always been present in Chinese society (with secret societies, 'bandits of honour', Taiping, the Boxers, etc.). These revolutionary rebels – a slightly grander version of the Red Guards, or convinced Maoists if you like – set themselves up nearly everywhere in the country, and even went so far as to make a stand against suspect Party administrations, suspected, that is, of lukewarmness towards the Cultural Revolution. They took possession of local radio stations and other propaganda outlets, and simply put themselves in the places of all the 'lukewarm' officials. In the general confusion, the opposition in some areas managed to set up cells of revolutionary rebels, which simply added to the chaos.

The army was quick to assess the situation, as shown by two strongly-worded editorials on 12 and 14 January 1967. On 13 January the formation was announced of a committee of the Cultural Revolution for the armed forces – with 18 members, led by a marshal – selected by the military committee of the Party. It was directly under the authority of the Party itself and of the national committee of the Cultural Revolution: a group which, though of course it has no official status is still (in the spring of 1969) calling the tune in Chinese political life, rather than leaving it to the Party's political office. It may be recalled here that those who constituted it had been Mao's brains trust in the past in Yenan (Lin Piao, Kang Sheng, Chen Po-ta, etc.). So the army was now subject at once to the Minister of Defence, Marshal Lin Piao, to Chen Po-ta (chief editor of the *Red Flag*) and to Madame Mao: a curious situation indeed. However, for the army, the time had come to act: the moment seemed propitious since there were provinces where the opposition was besieging the Maoist revolutionary rebels. So the People's Army, which up to then had managed to maintain a certain neutrality, despite the fact that its chief had been monopolizing the political scene since October 1966, now entered the arena of the Cultural Revolution. The army justified its intervention in its daily paper:

In the present situation of the great proletarian Cultural Revolution, it is not possible for the People's Army of Liberation to avoid intervening. There are some who would prefer non-intervention, but that is merely a pretext for annihilating the masses. There can no longer be compromise or neutrality: our People's Army must clearly and actively support the revolutionary and proletarian left.

(*Jiefangjun Bao*, 25 January 1967)

Thenceforth the army's fate was to be indissolubly linked with that of the Cultural Revolution, and the forces took the situation in hand. All over China, round public buildings, the Central Committee offices, the post and telecommunications network, the army established itself. It was a decisive intervention, for it enabled the Maoists to seize power at the local level by purging all Party committees and town councils hostile to the Cultural Revolution. But this interference in political life was not without its dangers to the fragile unity among the armed forces. Their increasing power everywhere soon became obvious to all: the People's Army became established in the administration, took over the supervision of the police, moved in on businesses and helped to run and organize them. The Cultural Revolution was entering a new phase: the Triple Alliance (February to May 1967).

The Triple Alliance

Under cover of the movement of the Triple Alliance (a union of the armed forces, the really revolutionary Party cadres, and revolutionary rebels whether Party members or not) of which it was certainly the most dynamic element, the army established revolutionary committees everywhere to take the place of the existing municipal councils. Thus, at every level, from the centre to the furthest provinces, revolutionary committees were gradually being formed which were entirely dedicated to the cause of the Cultural Revolution. In general, the older Party members stood for experience and moderation, while the young added revolutionary fervour, and the certainty that things would continue to progress. The army was hard put to it to arbitrate between the two camps. Events like those in Wuhan in July 1967 (with its 2 million people, it is a major military and strategic point, the centre of a network of roads, railways, ports, and major industry) were highly significant. The military authorities, under the command of General Chen Tsai-tao, who had taken over almost all authority in Hupeh province, had not as yet managed to put the Triple Alliance into effect; the Minister of Security, General Hsieh Fu-chi, President of the Revolutionary Committee of Peking and Vice-President of the Cultural Revolution Group in the army, arrived there, together with Wang Li, the Party's chief propagandist. The day they arrived, the two men from Peking were arrested by Unit 1802, under the command of the military governor-general of the province. By the 21 July, warships and airborne troops had been sent by Government. The two prisoners, thus liberated, were allowed to leave Wuhan the next day. On 25 July they received a triumphal reception from Marshal Lin Piao in Tien An Men Square, in front of a million demonstrators – which indicates the great scale of the incident! Inevitably General Chen Tsai-tao, the local commandant, was arrested, and his adjutant, General Liu Feng, hastened to declare his own loyalty to Mao. The whole Wuhan incident provided further fuel for attacking the 'protector', i.e., the President of the Republic, and also of course the two military chiefs who had been dismissed before. The Party's doctrinal review declared categorically: 'Peng Teh-huai and Lo Jui-ching, with the support of a very highly placed authority who has chosen the path of capitalism, have built up their personal reputation, recruited deserters and taken on rebels, formed factions to work for private interests, formed illegal connections with foreign countries, and conspired to usurp the power of the Party and the army.'* Wuhan was not unique among the tremendous upheavals taking place in China; similar situations were occurring elsewhere, and there were innumerable incidents in other provinces. Indeed, how could it be otherwise in a country 5,000 kilometres from north to south, and 4,000 from east to west? A country, furthermore, which had traditionally been divided into separate fiefs. After all, it is not so long since the time when the Central Government of Nanking could only preserve political unity by dint of permanent negotiating. But incidents such as this could be taken as warning signals: Peking must do nothing to threaten the positions won by the military leaders. Was China now, after twenty years of the new regime, to be carried back by the Cultural Revolution to the old battles between the warlords of the Middle Empire?

The Time for Compromise

The 'de-escalation' of the Cultural Revolution marked the time for compromise. And, as the months passed, the army's political capacity for catalysing the revolutionary rebels with the Party cadres became more doubtful. Yet out of that Triple Alliance there must somehow be formed the Party without which no Communist regime can function at all. The editorials in the Peking papers on 1 January 1968 spoke of the major tasks for the coming year, and for the first time were unambiguous in defining the Cultural Revolution as a 'great movement for remodelling the Communist Party'.

Thus the 're-launching' of the Triple Alliance during 1968 was to mark a return to a traditional Communist Party. Though nothing could be more opposed to the Cultural Revolution than any idea of compromise, there were compromises – in good

* *Hongqi*, 31 July 1967.

Chinese tradition – which eased the path for a number of returns to the fold, and especially that of the expelled cadres. However, the opposition still continued to be unmasked: for instance, General Yang Cheng-wu who had been acting Chief of the General Staff since the dismissal of General Lo Jui-ching in the summer of 1966, was dismissed in his turn on 28 March 1968, at the same time as Yu Li-chin, Political Commissar of the air force, and General Fu Chong-pi, Commander of the Peking garrison.

Since the fall of the Chief of the General Staff coincided with the glorification of Chiang Ching (Madame Mao), as illustrated by the slogan: 'Defend her to the death', this appeared to be a victory over the moderates who had made her the target of their attack. The dismissed Chief of the General Staff was also accused, with his supporters, of having attempted to overthrow the revolutionary committee in Peking. Forty-eight hours after his departure, the three official news organs – the Peking daily, *Renmin Ribao*, the army daily, *Jiefangjun Bao*, and the Party's doctrinal review, *Hongqi* – published identical editorials confirming that supreme authority was invested in the 'Revolutionary committees of the Triple Alliance' (30 March 1968). And the Shanghai daily made a point of recalling that the Party must command the gun, and not the other way round (*Wen Hui Bao*, 21 April 1968).

The army did not rejoice over the blow it had received: there was friction between military leaders and the Maoist authorities – so much so indeed that, for instance, in three provinces (Anhwei, Hunan and Yunnan) the leadership of the revolutionary committee had to be protected by troops drawn from outside the area concerned. It was certainly significant that the Government had to wait until 4 June to announce the name of the new Chief of the General Staff. And, it was with the deliberate design of reassuring the armed forces that the Government finally chose for that post a man universally respected, General Huang Yung-cheng, a veteran of the Chinese revolution, a deputy member of the Central Committee, and Commandant of the military district of Canton.

As the weeks went by, the tension slackened, thus making it

easier to form revolutionary committees in the provinces; but it was still a slow and hard victory, with twenty months of incessant struggle elapsing between the formation of the first such committee (Heilungkiang, 31 January 1967) and the last (Sinkiang, 5 September 1968). The Middle Empire saw continual wranglings and disputes: during one of the greatest periods of China's history, the first hundred and fifty years of the Tang dynasty, not a single hereditary prince mounted his throne unopposed; clearly, this tendency was far from being forgotten. Indeed, an editorial in the Heilungkiang provincial daily – that province being a microcosm of the Cultural Revolution in China – considered it expedient to point out that '... the creation of a revolutionary committee by no means indicates the end of the struggle between two political lines, two possible paths. The take-over of power in our provinces does not mean that the objective of the Cultural Revolution has yet been achieved ...' (15 February 1968).

The members of the revolutionary committees were not always in total harmony – far from it! Those who had previously been purged were now demanding to be restored in the name of the liberalization policy. The revolutionary rebels, on the other hand, were fighting to regain the power they had had in 1966, and loudly demanding a firm left-wing stand. Caught between the crossfire of right and left, the army finally won everyone's agreement by establishing its members in key posts in the provincial revolutionary committees, and of course, at lower levels as well. Thus the list which appeared in the Peking press of the leaders of the 28 revolutionary committees indicated that the 28 presidents consisted of 27 military men (17 generals, mainly commandants of military districts, and 10 army political commissars) as against one civilian. The army, omnipotent and omnipresent, certainly had the lion's share in the newly reconstituted administrative bodies of the country.

Towards the New Order

Thus, within days of the nineteenth anniversary of the establishment of the regime, people's China was fully supplied with revolutionary committees – committees whose importance cannot be overestimated since, for the moment at least, they are the essential organ of local power and government as well as being the official link between the provinces and the central government in Peking. At the same time, they also represent a tremendous simplification of structure in the People's Republic as compared with the cumbersome administrative edifice set up by the Constitution of 1954; for there is now no difference between Party and State bodies anywhere in the country. Thus, no reorganization of the machinery of state in red China could be undertaken without first reorganizing the Party hierarchy, and seriously involving the whole of the armed forces. Would, therefore, the convocation of the Ninth National Congress of the Communist Party (due to take place by statute ever since 1961, as each Congress had a mandate for only five years,* and the Eighth had been held in September 1956) be a curtain-raiser for a meeting of the People's National Assembly, whose term expired in the Autumn of 1968? The 3,037 deputies elected in September 1964 to the third National Assembly (this number was twice as large as had sat in the two previous assemblies in response 'to the development of socialist structures') ultimately sat no more than once (21 December 1964 to 4 January 1965) during its term of office – a clear violation of the Constitution which called for one session per year.† A similarly lackadaisical attitude was evinced in regard to the rules of the Party, as witness the non-convocation of the Central Committee plenum, and the non-reelection of the members who had been elected for five years in 1956.‡

* Article 31. 'The National Congress of the Party is elected for a term of five years . . . A session of the Party National Congress is to be convoked once a year by the Central Committee.'

† Article 25. 'The National Assembly of representatives of the Chinese people sits once a year when summoned by the permanent Committee. The National Assembly may hold an extraordinary session if the permanent Committee judges it necessary, or if it is proposed by one-fifth of the deputies.'

‡ Article 36. 'The Central Committee shall meet in plenary session at least twice a year, the session being convoked by the political office of the Central Committee.' Article 33. 'The Central Committee of the Party is elected for a term of five years.'

Since this situation, if prolonged, might be harmful to the whole country, it was important to remedy it as soon as possible. The 12th plenum of the Central Committee, which met from 13 to 31 October 1968, with the addition of the Group from the Central Committee responsible for the Cultural Revolution, the leaders of the provincial revolutionary committees, and certain high-ranking officers from the armed forces, were to take some extremely important measures. First and foremost was the dismissal of Liu Shao-chi, now actually mentioned by name in a long official communiqué: '. . . in witness of its intense revolutionary indignation over the counter-revolutionary crimes of Liu Shao-chi, the plenum has unaminously adopted the following resolution: to exclude Liu Shao-chi permanently from the Party, relieve him of all his functions, both inside the Party and outside it, and to continue to deplore the crimes he and his supporters have perpetrated which have been a betrayal of both the Party and the Nation. . . .' Though Liu Shao-chi could, as a member of the Communist Party Central Committee, be expelled, in an emergency, by a two-thirds majority, in conformity with article 16 of the Party statutes,* the plenary session had in fact violated the said statutes in not hearing the man's statement of his own case, which article 17 obliges it to do.† And further, as President of the Republic, legally and unanimously re-elected for four years on 3 January 1965, he could not constitutionally be replaced until his successor had been elected: the Constitution is clear on that point.‡

The other major decision taken by the plenum was obviously

---

* Article 16. 'Any decision to remove a member or deputy from the Central Committee of the C.P. must be taken by the Party National Congress. In an emergency, such a decision may be taken by a two-thirds majority of the Central Committee plenary session, but it must then be ratified at the next session of the Party National Congress.'

† Article 17. 'Expulsion from the Party is the harshest of all disciplinary measures that can be taken within the Party. In making or ratifying such a decision, all Party organizations must act with the utmost prudence, examining and studying in detail all the facts and material evidence in the case, and attentively listening to the defence of himself given by the person concerned.'

‡ Article 45. 'The President and Vice-President of the Republic of China will carry out their functions up to the moment when the new President and Vice-President elected by the next National Assembly take over from them.'

the announcement of the forthcoming convocation of the Ninth Congress: 'The plenum considers that, despite the storms of this great revolution, suitable conditions now prevail on the ideological, political and organizational levels for holding the Ninth Congress of the Chinese Communist Party. The plenum has decreed that this should be convoked at the earliest opportune moment.'

Finally, on 1 April 1969, the long-awaited Ninth Congress met – having been due since 1961, and described by Hsinhua, the official press agency, as 'the greatest in Party history'.

After the ten past years of difficulty in collegial leadership, with Mao as President of the Party, and Liu Chao-chi President of the Republic, we now see a return to the kind of unified leadership that existed before 1958. Once again, it was a new development in the total pattern of Chinese thinking: the need to see the country embodied in one man, an individual honoured by the entire country. The Cultural Revolution having thus provoked a crisis – intended, directed and resolved by Mao himself – the session of the Ninth Congress, 'the Congress of unity and victory', as the Hsinhua agency defined it, was thus the consecration and apotheosis of Mao's victory.

It will however call for some time spent watching men and events to discover just what the changes wrought in red China by the 1,512 delegates to the Ninth Congress really amount to.

If, contrary to all expectations, persuasion and propaganda (the regime's standard methods), and the continuance not of civil war proper, but of miniature civil wars among local factions in the provinces, prevent the achievement of the New Order, then, though it is not by any means his chosen weapon, Mao will be obliged to make use of force. But to make such a decision would indicate the inadequacy of the principle he himself has declared ultimate – that the gun must always come second to the Party.

Dragon or Bogeyman?

The question no one can avoid asking is: is red China really aggressive or not? Before attempting to consider an answer, it may be worth recalling that, twenty-five centuries before Clausewitz, Sun Tse, China's most magnificent strategist, stated the principle that a good general must, first and foremost, be a past master in the art of deceiving the enemy. Far from having developed beyond this, Mao's 'thoughts' would seem to start from that idea. So it appears that there is no possibility of answering the question of China's aggressiveness.

However, it is important to recognize the fact that this vast dragon with its cruel claws can not move very far. Indeed the Chinese armed forces have quite a number of weak points. They are certainly, from the point of view of the rest of Asia, an element of force upon which Peking can rely to develop its policies, but they could not possibly attempt any operations outside their own borders. Though red China certainly has a large fighting potential, it is very ill-balanced. Nor should we forget the age of the military leaders, all of them veterans of the heroic days of Yenan. Their minds still revolve round the notion of guerrilla warfare, and their prudence is such as to make them little inclined for change. Furthermore, as in all armies, there are causes for discontent: for instance, the long periods of separation from family, the ban on marriage; and there are also a lot of soldiers who would prefer to devote less time to studying politics and more to military matters. However, all this is far from amounting to the general restlessness in the forces which some people claim to discern.

Then, too, the most significant characteristic of all the Chinese forces is the way they are deployed. Though the precise figures are kept secret, it is certainly quite sure that there is no large concentration of troops on the North Vietnam border. To Peking, the most important strategic areas are, and remain, the industrial sector of the north-east (where there are munitions factories built underground in the mountains, as well as underground arms depots), the areas opposite Taiwan (Formosa) and the Russian frontier. Thus, China's forces are deployed in what is essentially a defensive manner. With few motor vehicles, and a not very adequate railway network, the ground forces are not very mobile strategically (since regional and militia groups are by definition restricted in movement). The airborne force would also seem to be deployed defensively: its very composition indicates that the Chinese air force has the most limited capacity for attack (in support of the land forces). And as for the navy, its mission at present is to defend the coastline, and protect shipping in China's territorial waters; the only unknown factor here is the operational capability of the submarine fleet.

Clearly, then, the Chinese armed forces are so arranged as to be pre-eminently defensive in purpose: so for the moment there is no immediate threat: In short, though these forces have a lot on their side when it comes to defence, they have, on the other hand, despite their huge size, very little capacity for attack – which in fact logically reflects both the military and the political thinking of China concerning the function of the army. That thinking we know from the writings of Mao, the directives of Marshal Lin Piao, and the documents put out by the military-affairs commission of the Central Committee: China is today the only country in the world which has officially and deliberately admitted that its war will take place on its own territory – with all the sacrifices and destruction that situation necessarily implies. Marshal Lin Piao gave a speech on the subject, which has at least the merit of complete clarity: 'It is necessary to lead the enemy to penetrate deep into our territory. Only by letting him come to us can we force him to disperse his troops, so as to have him by every finger, and bog down his legs. Then, unit by unit, mouthful by mouthful, we shall be able to dispose of him. . . .' (3 September, 1965.)

Heavy forces would only be brought in later, with the ubiquity of the Militia providing strategic mobility, and the autarchic organization of the people's communes – so many units of survival – compensating for the disruption of administrative liaison and communications in general. The war would have to be long: hence the need for the armed forces and for the people of China to have the kind of unwavering motivation and discipline which the Cultural Revolution is working to create in a situation of peace.

So, by drawing the qualitative maximum from her greatest quantitative advantage – people – China, invulnerable within her own 'sanctuary', none the less, for the present at least, has a very limited area for manoeuvre consisting geographically of her own territory and that of her immediate neighbours.

The Detonator of the 'Great Upheaval'

Thus, though the capacity of the Chinese armed forces for attack is at the moment small, it is not non-existent. And to its immediate neighbours, Peking's army represents a real threat, for it would be quite powerful enough to achieve simple and spectacular successes in terms of infiltration by foot-soldiers in any but the most open countryside. Even though it might never be put into effect, such a threat could be enough to obtain far from negligible advantages of a political kind without there being any need actually to enlarge the area of operation. India, for instance, has had bitter experience of this. Peking, which has never agreed the boundaries imposed upon it by force by the 'imperialist' States, has always declared itself to be acting for the perfectly legitimate recovery of its own property, where India is concerned. The Himalayan conflict (extremely limited in time, space and, even more so, in the number of troops involved) in the autumn of 1962 gave us an indication of what people's China can do when circumstances seem propitious. Thus, to protect its irredentist policy in Tibet, Peking systematically opposes the U.S.S.R. (which is trying to support an independent India to provide a counterbalance to China in south-east Asia). It is Moscow's desire to foster agreement between India and Pakistan, so as to help both to become indifferent to the lures of China, and it has been interesting to watch Moscow moving from an almost exclusively pro-Indian policy to one of balance between New Delhi and Rawalpindi: the Kashmir conflict opened the way to the change by providing a pretext for supplying Pakistan with Russian arms in June and July 1968.

As for the U.S.S.R., by invoking the 'unfair treaties' between Tsarist Russia and imperial China (Aigun in 1858, Peking in 1860 and St Petersburg in 1881), the Chinese leaders began questioning afresh the present Sino-Soviet boundary (some 10,400 kilometres long). China wants her lost territory back. As Mao has explained: 'The Soviet Union, under pretext of securing Mongolia's independence, actually brought that country under her own domination. . . . A hundred years ago, the area east of Baikal became Russian territory, and since then, Vladivostock, Khabarovsk, Kamchatka and other places have been Soviet land. We have not yet presented our note to this effect. . . .'* The Chinese, whether Maoist or not, are keeping a close watch on the vast stretches of Siberia which extend to infinity before them, a land of promise. The areas in dispute are not inhabited by Russians – apart, of course from Siberia, where the imperial dream of a march to the East (which the present occupants of the Kremlin inherit, whatever Marx might have said, and in which they are pursuing the achievement begun by Khrushchev) has resulted in the forced transportation of millions of young people from Russia and the Ukraine, whose job is to carry out Moscow's programme of 'Russifying' those areas, with the hearts of pioneers and the fervour of crusaders. But then, they are not inhabited by Chinese either. However, neither Moscow nor Peking has suggested that settlers there should have any right of self-determination, though that was Lenin's express intention (and both claim to be inspired by him!); indeed, he even envisaged the possible secession of the new State they might form. Thus, the Sino-Soviet boundary dispute, latent since 1960, causes minor but fairly continuous incidents (over seven thousand up to the present), and clearly proletarian internationalism has not managed to overcome nationalist interest. But there is no real threat of conflict there, for the logistic conditions which would favour the Chinese in the East of Mongolia would equally apply to the Soviets in the west: anyone therefore in trouble with the Chinese would obviously try to restore the balance by seeking aid from the Russians and *vice versa*. And, at present, Peking is certainly not prepared for a generalized war. China's attacks, all of them verbal, and each more fierce than the last, are primarily an indication of the Chinese leaders' determination to prevent the Soviets' attempts to subvert any local nationalist groups and thus lead to the establishment of more or less independent entities. To expect to see mechanized units and vast numbers of troops moving through Sinkiang to

* Speech of 10 July 1964.

the Russian border is a mirage which could not possibly materialize for a very long time. In any case, no one in Peking seriously envisages winning back the lost territories by military means.

As for the small nations bordering on the people's Republic, which have for longer or shorter periods in their history been wholly or partially tributary states of the Middle Empire, Peking is at the moment laying no claim to them. But the Chinese army could, in fact, act effectively there if it wished: on the borders of Burma, of Thailand, of Laos, and even of Cambodia, for instance, it could act as it did in Korea when MacArthur, declaring that Peking would never move, made the major error of crossing the 38th parallel and advancing to the Yalu. For the first time in two hundred years, the Chinese army moved outside its own frontiers, under the command of General Lin Piao, to hold in check the world's greatest military power, a power possessing nuclear weapons, and repel them by forced marches to a point more than 100 kilometres south of the 38th parallel. At present China feels no need to expand: the lack of any reaction on Peking's part to the bloody events in Indonesia in September 1965, which led to the destruction of her faithful and powerful ally, the Indonesian Communist Party, makes that eminently clear.

But though the gigantic dragon with the sharp claws is not yet ready to leap from its lair, it remains a cause for disquiet, and the disquiet has become something more or less worldwide since, now that the dragon has nuclear teeth, it could, with a single thoughtless move, become the detonator of a worldwide catastrophe.

FIVE. THE NUCLEAR CHALLENGE

The atom bomb, which the American reactionaries use to frighten people with, is a paper tiger. It looks terrifying, but in reality it is not. It is, of course, a weapon that can cause vast massacres, but it is people who determine the result of a war, and not one or two new weapons.

Mao Tse-tung

Imperial China, from the fifteenth century onwards, sought refuge in literature and despised science, and it died for failing to understand that no civilization can exist or survive unless it is supported by technological, scientific, military and economic progress. Mao the scholar has not forgotten this lesson from history, and thus, ever since the proclamation of the people's Republic, all his efforts have gone to providing red China with that terrible white man's weapon which had been tested twice on yellow populations four years earlier, at Hiroshima and Nagasaki.

Challenge against Challenge

The reason for China's scientific policy is her own determination to create one. It is the result of a series of successive 'challenges' which Peking has had to face and cope with: the challenge to its security (people's China is ringed round with American bases, and subject to a total embargo by the United States which gives its full support to Taiwan (Formosa)); the challenge to its dignity (though its population is a quarter of the human race, people's China is excluded from the United Nations); the challenge to its prestige (as an Asian state and major world power, people's China does not intend to be left out when Asian problems are under discussion, or matters relating to arms control or even disarmament). The very foundations of Chinese life and civilization are at stake – it is literally a matter of life and death. That is why Mao, once established in Peking, mobilized everything – resources, intelligence, activity (universities, industries, and so on) – on a national scale. Stalin provided the example: a great state with a totalitarian government can mobilize all its resources and thus achieve definite technological objectives. And it was by this means that Chinese scientists and engineers were to respond to the nuclear challenge of the white world, and, in record time, make people's China the world's third thermo-nuclear power. The modernizers at the end of the nineteenth century made their battle cry, 'to enrich the country and make it powerful', and Mao has made it his own. Once again, China follows the path of renewal with continuity. Now the mighty sharp-clawed dragon has nuclear teeth. Now, with her bombs, China has two forms of military power: an atomic arsenal has been added to the sheer weight of numbers. No one can doubt China's determination to be recognized and respected. Now, twenty years after recovering her sense of national greatness and military power, people's China, free of the shackles other countries have always previously laid upon her, can today throw out a new challenge – this time a nuclear one. And, though without Russian help she could never have developed her nuclear capacity with anything like the speed she has, she has now reached the point of trying to oust Russia from her place as the chief scientific nation in the socialist world, just as she is disputing her 'leadership' in Communism. Certainly the dizzying speed with which China's scientific policy has expanded (its origin, its development, and its future) calls for our careful attention; for, ultimately, it must affect the fate of all mankind.

Training Abroad and Returning Home

After one hundred and fifty years of weakness and foreign domination, and forty years of civil and international wars which destroyed her economy and decimated her population, China – whose modernization under Western influence was limited to six regions, almost all of them round the coast, and containing barely 10 per cent of the population – was a backward and underdeveloped continent when the Communists came to power in 1949. Though its remarkable scientific development had made it continually in advance of the West without a break from the fifth century B.C. to the fifteenth A.D., the China of twenty years ago had barely more than a hundred thousand professionally trained people (7,000 doctors, 10,000 agriculturalists, 10,000 scientists, 25,000 engineers and 60,000 lawyers), with the addition of a significant body of several thousands of foreign experts.

Certain names stand out. For instance, Chien San-chiang (born 1907), descended from a Chinese literary family, graduated from Peking University and went to France with a letter of recommendation from the famous mathematician Hsiung Ching-lai, a professor at Peking and a friend of Henri Poincaré and Paul Painlevé; the letter was addressed to Paul Langevin who, in 1934, accepted him in the Joliot-Curie laboratories. There he worked as assistant in the Radium Institute, and followed Frédéric Joliot-Curie in the Collège de France. Professor Chien San-chiang (who at that time wrote his name as Tsen San-tiang) met in Paris, in 1937, a Chinese woman doctor Ho Zah-wei (sometimes known as To Tse-hui, which is the Japanese pronunciation), who was on her way back from Heidelberg University, and she later became his wife. He got his doctorate in science from Paris University in 1943 (and was in 1946 to win the Henri de Barville prize from the Paris Academy of Sciences); he was forced, together with his wife, to stay in Paris when the war came, and continued there teaching in the Sorbonne. The Germans took great interest in his work and sought his collaboration: Admiral Wilhelm Canaris, Director of Germany's military intelligence service, went himself to Paris to meet him at the Hotel Lutetia, where the Abwehr services were established. He invited him to go to the Kaiser Wilhelm Institute in Berlin to work with Otto Hahn (who was to win the Nobel prize for chemistry in 1945). The invitation was politely refused, and the Admiral did not press it. However, Chien instead made contact with the resistance, and also with Captain John Wilson of the Intelligence Service, in Meaux, to whom he gave a memorandum about his work. A copy went to Russia, where it was so useful that, twenty years later, the

Chinese were to say that the help they then got from the U.S.S.R. was no more than a fair reward for the services Chien San-chiang had rendered the Allies in the war. After the victory of the Chinese Communists, Chien San-chiang left France to return to Peking – with Joliot-Curie's full approval. He then went to Russia to meet his Soviet colleagues: the well-known professor, Igor Kourtchakov, and his assistant, Professor Iakob Dorfmann, in Atomgrad 2, on the banks of Lake Baikal, before finally settling in Peking. The Chinese atomic scientist, Tang Pa-chek, told his colleagues in the international Atomic Energy Agency in Vienna in confidence (always the best form of publicity) that Mao had one day summoned Chien San-chiang and told him that China's highest interests demanded that she have her own atom bomb by 1 January 1965. Chien was two months ahead of time: the first Chinese A-bomb was exploded on 14 October 1964. Professor Chien San-chiang, Director of the Chinese Institute of Atomic Studies, is pursuing his researches now into both peaceful and military uses of nuclear energy. His wife is the chief of the cyclotron laboratory in the Peking Institute of Atomic Energy.

The father of Chinese rocketry, Professor Chien Hsueh-chien (born 1912), one – possibly the greatest – of the world's few specialists in nuclear propulsion, had an equally chequered career. A colonel in the American Air Force, Director of the missile section of the scientific commission of National Defence, Consultant to the U.S. Navy, he was appointed to the Chair of Jet Propulsion at the California Institute of Technology (Caltech) – which also gave him a doctorate – and remained there until 1955. In 1947, Professor Chien Hsueh-chien spent some time in West Germany, studying German rocket techniques, but returned immediately to the U.S.A. In 1955, as a result of negotiations in Geneva as secret as they were bizarre, it was decided between the American and Chinese delegates that the Chinese expert be 'expelled' from the United States. The day after he left, Wernher von Braun was to say of him: 'He will be my greatest adversary.' From a man with as little modesty as von Braun that was quite a compliment! Almost as soon as he got home, having become a member of the Academy of Sciences,

Professor Chien Hsueh-chien took over the directorship of the Institute of Dynamics. We all know what followed: on 27 October 1966, the Lop Nor nuclear rocket exploded on target.

At the same time as the fathers of the bomb and the rocket were leaving their training grounds in the West, Professor Wang Kan-chang, who had been educated in the German laboratories of the supreme father of the atomic era, Otto Hahn, went to teach physics in the great American 'nuclear' university of Berkeley. From there he went to Russia (from 1956 to 1961), becoming Associate Director of the Institute of Soviet Nuclear Research in Dubna, one of the largest centres of nuclear physics in the world (as the common creation of all the socialist countries except Albania, it was by statute outside the Soviet nuclear programme). He then returned to Peking, and became Joint-Director of the Institute of Atomic Energy there.

We may also recall Professor Chao Chung-yao, a nuclear physicist, also from Caltech. Having worked in the universities of Hall and Harvard, he left America for Peking, where he became vice-Director of the Institute of Atomic Energy. From 1956 to 1961, the Professor went to Dubna for further training, and it was he who discovered gamma rays.

Also from British and American universities, we find Professors Peng Huang-wu and Yang Li-ming, and Professor Chan Chia-hua, Vice-President of the Chinese Academy of Sciences, specializing in uranium and radioactive metals, Professor Li Su-kuang, also Professor Wu Yu-sun, China's representative in negotiating scientific agreements with the socialist world. We may also mention Professor Chu Hung-yuan, who was in Moscow-Dubna from 1956 to 1961; Professor Cheng Wen-yu in the Peking Institute of Atomic Energy; Professor Chang Tsung-sui, Professor of Nuclear Physics in Peking. Other doctors from Western universities include Professor Hu Ning, Professor Tai Chuan-tsen and Professor Teng Chia-hsien.

Among Chinese experts involved in the rocket-research programme, as well as Professor Chien Hsueh-chien, two outstanding names are Professor Kuo Yung-huai (Caltech) and Professor Shen Yuan (Imperial College, London).

Though on an entirely different level, Soviet assistance is far from negligible. Of the 11,000 experts sent to China by the Kremlin, only 4 per cent were noteworthy scientists, but, on the other hand, they did play a major part as teachers and technical advisers in the various Chinese institutes of research and education. And in addition, as Mikhail Suslov, the Kremlin's chief ideologist noted in his report of 14 February 1964, 1,300 teachers and 7,500 students (5,500 of them post-graduate) went from China to complete their training in Russia. In July and August 1960, the Russians left China, and the Chinese left Russia. But since then, Chinese nuclear scientists have not hesitated to travel to universities and research centres all over the free world to increase their qualifications. Thus, there were several thousand Chinese students in American universities during the academic year 1966–7. Other figures appear in the following table:

Chinese Science Students

Europe	Asia	Canada	Latin America	Africa
5,198 – of whom:	19,427 – of whom:	3,306	3,508	2,213
1,308 U.K.	5,353 China			
60 Germany	4,628 India			
539 Turkey	1,249 Japan			
536 France	others			
others				

(Figures from the O.E.C.D., published Paris 1968, *Politiques nationales de la science: États-Unis*, p. 337)

In Denmark, for instance, young Chinese scientists of an extremely high standard, we are told, come in regular succession to work in Professor Aage Bohr's laboratories (the Danish scholar Niels Bohr is the father of modern nuclear physics), in the Blegdamsvej centre of the Institute of Theoretical Physics in Copenhagen.

However, not all the Chinese experts come home to their own country. According to Kuo Mo-jo, President of the Academy of Sciences, there are some 10,000 still living outside China, 4,000 of them, aged between thirty-five and forty-five, in universities or research centres in the U.S.A. Those who have returned, a far from negligible proportion of those most competent in both teaching and research, are bringing the new regime great advantages: we can see the results today.

Scientific Planning and Reorientation

By putting into effect a firm policy whose methods and scope it would be dangerous to underestimate – a policy which grows out of the slogan: 'The three supports of the Revolution are the class struggle, the struggle for production and the struggle for scientific experimentation' – people's China will, in twenty years' time, if it continues at its present fantastic pace, possess a body of scientific and technological experts which can bear comparison with any in the most scientifically advanced countries. China's scientific 'leap forward' is thus starting off with a group of about 2,000 scholars and researchers, about 80 per cent of whom have received all their training abroad. In the four years from 1949 to 1953, the Academy of Sciences was to become the centre of research and development for Chinese science. After the launching of the first five-year plan (1953–7), the Academy of Sciences, reorganized under the guidance of some dozen Soviet advisers, was then closely modelled on the corresponding body in Moscow.

But who was to determine scientific policy? The Chinese Communist Party had no scientific or technological experts among its cadres; and those Chinese who had come back from the West in order to take part in the 'building of socialism' had come far more out of patriotism than any strictly Communist ideal. Yet another of those 'contradictions' which Mao sees at the heart of his teaching and thinking! Perhaps, but a 'contradiction' of that kind could hardly fail to disturb the Party leaders. However, since they were not yet ready to take over, the Party was obliged, against the grain, to leave the directing of science to the scientists. And Yu Kuang-yuan, head of the Scientific Division of the Propaganda Department of the Central Committee, recognized with some bitterness at the Eighth Party Congress that: 'to direct scientific work, the Party has to trust wholly to the scientists. Modern sciences have many branches, and only specialists can know the details of each. When we are faced with scientific problems, we must be ready to learn humbly from our specialists.'* However, 'Leave science to the scientists' was a slogan not readily accepted in the Communist world; and by the time it held its second plenary session, in May 1957, the Academy of Sciences had already lost its leading position in determining Chinese policy in regard to things scientific. With the 'liberalization' promised in his so-called 'Hundred Flowers' speech in 1956, Mao rather rashly unleashed a democratic movement within a dictatorship which was soon to become something rather different. What happened was that the campaign urging all Chinese to express their criticisms frankly, was transformed in a matter of weeks, and contrary to all expectations, into a general outburst of dissatisfaction with and hostility to Communist methods. Reaction was inevitable: it took the form of a movement against all non-Communist groups, which affected every province and every element of society. The Party then took total control of all scientific activities, strictly subordinating them to the needs of the economy and of national defence. On 23 November 1958, an all-powerful Scientific and Technological Commission was set up, responsible solely and directly to the Government. Chaired by Marshal Nieh Jung-chen, deputy Prime Minister and a member of the Central Committee, it included a number of leading Communists, but not a single first-class scientist. The Marshal justified this monolithic control in terms of the ideological situation in the party:

If we allow science to follow the road envisaged by middle-class experts, the scientific work of our country will be completely divorced from its political function in the building-up of socialism. ... Thus, the Party's total control over science and technology is the fundamental guarantee of the superiority of socialism, and of the rapid development of our scientific techniques. ... Those who maintain that laymen cannot guide the experts are adopting a position

* Session of 26 September 1956.

contrary to the principle that the political leadership is supreme. There can be no scientific progress outside the guidance of the party.*

This direct intrusion of ideology into science was, however, as nothing compared with what happened in Russia when Stalin forced his scholars to adopt Lysenko's theories on the inheritance of acquired characteristics, thus holding back biological progress for ten years! Furthermore, though henceforth it was every scientist's obligation to become 'red and competent' (note the order of priorities!), the experts themselves had no intention of being guided by Marxist–Leninist ideology. The Party was to be forced by circumstances to adopt a more liberal attitude to the scientists, and in fact to give them very much what they wanted. Concessions continued to increase, and from 1961 on, the Party's doctrinal journal took to defending ideas totally contrary to those it had maintained in 1958 and 1959. Marshal Chen Yi, Minister of Foreign Affairs, even went so far as to say:

There are some people who need time for their studies, and others who have little interest in politics and will give little time to political activity. Provided they produce results in their own field, and contribute to the construction of socialism, there should be no objection to their taking a lesser part in political activity. . . . One should not lay too much stress on family origins: young people born in the exploiting classes may well be revolutionaries . . . †

Following the position adopted by Professor Chien San-chiang, the top man in the Chinese atomic hierarchy, in which he was supported by Professor Chien Hsueh-chien, chief of the military scientific programme, scientists were permitted to follow a system known as the 'five-sixths': by this, despite the Marxist-Maoist dogma that the same principles apply to people in every situation, scientists were henceforth permitted to devote five-sixths of their time to research, and only one-sixth to political or administrative activities. Even better: professors were given the right to select their students on the basis of scientific ability alone; and both teachers and students were dispensed from the obligatory period of 'ruralization', which applied to all other intellectuals and even to the military. Thus,

* *Hongqi*, 1 October 1958.   † Speech, 10 August 1961.

quietly and without any major disputes, the scientists' demands were all satisfied. By a tacit agreement, the 'scientific mandarins' were kept happy. The final instance of this was the sixteen-point Decision of 8 August 1966 by the Party's Central Committee in regard to the Cultural Revolution, whereby they were left out of all the turbulence. Point 12: 'Policy towards scientists, technicians and their staffs' stated in so many words that 'special attention must be paid to men of science and other members of the scientific and technological world who have distinguished themselves by their work. As for their conception of the world and their style of working, we can help them to improve these things gradually.' In other words, the atom race must not be interrupted by political 'incidents'. In keeping scientists and technologists outside Party struggles and the Cultural Revolution, the Chinese leaders were really giving public expression to their determination to foster research by every possible means, and to give ever greater importance to scientific training. The planning for scientific research is the most striking illustration of this.

It was in fact on 29 January 1956 that Mao uttered an eloquent appeal to overcome China's backwardness in the fields of science and technology, a backwardness further stressed by the second five-year plan (1958–62) then in course of preparation. In order to achieve the 'march towards science', a planning committee for scientific development was immediately set up under Marshal Chen Yi, charged with establishing a twelve-year plan for scientific development (1956–67). In seven months, two hundred Chinese and seventy Russian scientists, led by A. J. Nikhailov, outlined a scientific plan to be presented to the Eighth Party Congress, where Liu Shao-chi, the Recorder, declared that this Chinese plan would 'bring [China] to the highest level in the world in the spheres of science and technology, so essential to the national economy'.* The plan was then submitted to Soviet specialists for examination – 26 study groups, composed of some 640 top Russian scientists, went through it with a fine tooth comb (we may recall that the Soviet nuclear programme was then in full swing: their A-bomb

* Session of 16 September 1956.

appeared in August 1949, and their H-bomb in August 1953); but it was not to be put into operation until a further examination had been made in collaboration with a politico-scientific delegation of 120 Chinese who went specially to Russia for the purpose. This dual negotiation was felt to be so important to Peking that Mao himself went to Moscow, for the second time in his life, from 2 to 21 November 1957.

Finally ratified by the National Assembly, the twelve-year plan covered the period from January 1956 to December 1967 – though its full text was never published by the Peking authorities. In fact, at least as far as one can judge from some parts of it that were published, particularly in university journals, this particular long-term plan was, like all Chinese plans, a fairly flexible guideline, putting forward general principles without going into great detail, but setting fairly definite time limits. Its purpose was, in short, to define major objectives, to foresee long-term needs, and give a certain direction to the training of specialists. The plan was also designed to develop science all over the country, envisaging that by 1967, eleven of the chief towns of China – Canton, Shanghai, Shenyang (formerly Mukden), Fushun, Harbin, Liuta (formerly Dairen), Nanking, Peking, Tientsin, Tsingtao, and Wuhan – should have modern research centres so that there could be coordinated work among, for instance, universities, scientific associations, and provincial delegations of the Academy of Sciences.

The Sino-Soviet discord over the application of certain articles in the secret Defence Treaty of 15 October 1957 (denounced in June 1969) did not prevent partial agreements from continuing in other fields, in particular that of the communal production of fissile materials. The break seems to have taken place in stages. It is clear that the Chinese continued to receive important information and direct scientific and technical aid to the 17 July 1960, the date when the Soviet technicians were called home, and all aid agreements cancelled. It was in fact at the plenum of the Russian Party's Central Committee, from 13 to 16 July 1960, that the decision was made: Peking was informed on 17 July. What was done could not be undone, but the Conference of the 81 Communist parties in

Moscow, in November 1960, was to delay the official announcement of the Moscow–Peking discord for three years. The twelve-year plan which was to extend from January 1956 to December 1967 was eventually replaced in 1963 by a new ten-year plan, to run from 1963 to 1972. There seems little doubt that the major purpose of this ten-year plan was to make sure that China would have long-range missiles by 1972 – and in fact the years 1970–72 were also pinpointed by General Pierre Gallois, the so-called inspirer of the deterrent forces in France, as the time when the nuclear threat of Peking would be unleashed on the world. Meanwhile, China's present nuclear ballistic arsenal is quite adequate to make it clear that the era of the West's absolute supremacy is past.

The Long March to Knowledge

In the past, once they had finished their Chinese university courses, the sons of the nobility, the middle class, and the scholars whom white men describe by the Portuguese term 'mandarins', used to leave for Europe or America to learn about the West, or, as they used to say in China then, 'to drink foreign ink'. That no longer happens: the young people now stay at home to achieve that 'Long March' to knowledge which Mao offers them. All of red China lives under the banner of education, from the kindergarten to the tomb. In fact the idea of spending one's life learning is a very traditional one in China: Confucius himself said, 'When his coffin is closed, then the wise man stops learning.' Today's Chinese is condemned to study for life: in kindergartens, primary schools, high schools, and universities, in the factories, in the fields, in the army!

Once again, Westerners have erred in applying their own ways of thought to China. They never would have thought there could be enough trained Chinese to give China the scientific and technological experts she needed to become a scientific power. Yet Chien Hsueh-chien and his colleague Kuo Yung, have, with their staff, managed in twelve years to train 400 researchers and some 1,000 engineers, who are now working on the production of intercontinental rockets. Twenty years after the start of the regime, people's China has some 18,000 highly trained, and 25,000 semi-skilled workers involved in scientific research – more than Great Britain. The increase in education, the high percentage who go on to further education, both boys and girls (in scientific research 30 per cent of all personnel are women; in the equivalent faculties in the universities – medicine, etc, – 1 in every 5 research students is a woman), makes it possible for everyone to follow the work done by the researchers, or at least to understand their purpose and their interest. And that is not the least of the results of the education being carried out on so vast a scale all over people's China.

Mao has laid a bet on the future by placing such stress on higher education. From the fall of the Manchu dynasty in 1911 until the coming of Mao in 1949 – thirty-eight years in all – there were all in all no more than 210,827 students receiving higher education in universities whose methods and programmes were based on the American pattern. In 1952 a total reform of higher education in people's China was undertaken: in future it was to be available in 239 establishments (18 traditional universities, 50 major polytechnics and institutes of technology, 39 schools of medicine, 34 agricultural institutes, 52 teachers' training colleges, and 46 other miscellaneous establishments). Two main centres of higher education emerged – Peking, with over 40 universities and institutes, granting some 25,000 degrees or diplomas per year, and Shanghai, turning out about 14,000 qualified students every academic year. From then on, higher education was to develop fantastically and, on 5 June 1964, it actually had its own special ministry created (there had been one formed in November 1952, but it was closed again in 1958); it was characterized by the coexistence of some twenty traditional universities, i.e., with a lot of different faculties, and over 200 major polytechnics and specialist institutions. The universities prepare their members to teach in higher and secondary education, and train students for scientific research. The polytechnics and specialist schools only train engineers and technologists for a particular sector (there is, for example, a petroleum institute, and another for geology, 'magnificently equipped', we are told by Professor Mendelssohn, the well-known Oxford physicist, who frequently visits China). Students who have qualified in electro-technics or electro-dynamics will round off their training with some nuclear studies; the programme will include mathematics, atomic physics, experimental methods in nuclear physics, protection from rays, and the interaction of atomic science with agriculture and medicine. A great many students who have specialized in working with radio-isotopes thus have a firm basis of knowledge about electronic equipment for nuclear physics and the techniques for the measurement and control of radiation. About a million students receive higher education – in other words only the most brilliant of the secondary pupils. There is a severely selective entrance examination: only one in ten pupils can be taken. In addition to this first hurdle, there is a fixed quota for each individual discipline, determined each year by the Government. Thus, though in theory one's choice of training is free, it is enormously restricted in practice by the number of places available. Furthermore, higher education is also to some extent the training of an elite: there are 100 million schoolchildren, and 9 million students – the figures speak for themselves! This is China's solution to the 'contradiction' between the need to educate the masses, and the need to give special training to those who must lead the way in the world of scientific advance.

A full university course lasts an average of five years. There was a time when this was reduced to three years, but the Government did not want 'cut-rate' specialists, and in 1955 the five-year course was restored. The 'third stage' is undergoing certain alterations. When it comes to research, there are 10,000 candidates applying for only 1,500 jobs. The best of these are sent to the subsidiary establishments so that they can act as live-wires there. But the mass of average scientists who have qualified in part-time colleges are drawn from the population as a whole. The university has also set on foot a most interesting system of re-training courses for ordinary factory and peasant engineers. It must be admitted, however, that those administering the educational system have not yet succeeded in solving the problems inherent in trying to create a cultured elite and a body of experts. The Central Committee of the Chinese Communist

Party, in its statement of 8 August 1966 on the Cultural Revolution, declared in its Point 10, 'The Reform of Education':

To reform the old system of education, as well as old principles and methods of teaching, is a task of enormous importance facing the great proletarian Cultural Revolution now taking place. The phenomenon of our teaching establishments being dominated by bourgeois intellectuals must disappear during the course of that great Cultural Revolution.

And Mao confirmed this by issuing a directive, published by all the Chinese press:

We must preserve the universities; by that I chiefly mean the technological and scientific universities. However, we must reduce the length of studies there, bring the revolution into education, put proletarian politics ahead of everything else, and follow the pattern established by the Shanghai machine-tool factory where the technological staff are trained from among the workers. Students must be chosen from among experienced peasants and workers, and sent back to productive work after a few years of study.*

A major – perhaps the essential – theme of the Cultural Revolution, the reform of education in China, is still too new for us to be able to analyse its repercussions. It would appear, however, that the coming of a second generation of researchers has made it possible for the regime to 're-deploy' the high-ranking scholars who have spent almost their entire career in the West, into administrative posts. The emergence of this new generation from the universities, the perfect product of Research and Development, has brought something new: participation. Factory workers and business technicians work together with the researchers to map out common research programmes. And while the technicians do training periods in laboratories, scientific advice is being given on the factory floor. We are far from being able to make any real comparison between the resources being put into R. and D. (Research and Development) in China and in the West, since we do not know the gross amount being paid in salaries to workers involved in this process. If one seeks to find the 'coefficient of research', in other words, what it is in terms of the G.N.P., we discover that it is 1·1 per cent (as against

* *Renmin Ribao*, 22 July 1968.

1·6 per cent in Japan, 3 per cent in Russia and 3·2 per cent in the U.S.A.) – but this is still fairly astounding if one recalls that people's China still needs to invest large sums in the base sector to ensure that the country develops its potential fully.

Any conclusions we come to can only be approximative, since many economists are still uncertain about just what role R. and D. play as a growth factor. And it is all the easier to understand their hesitation in that neither Japan, with the fastest growth-rate in the world, (and a competitor, even in electronics, with the U.S.A.), nor Italy, for all its prosperity, is illustrious for its scientific efforts – though both are growing so rapidly. Can there be said to be a direct link between growth-rate and the efforts devoted to research? It is an open question.

Today, then, higher education has produced some 1,160,000 graduates. In other words: five times more in the twenty years since the establishment of the regime than in the fifty years before. Young red China, dynamic and self-assured, gives the lie to the old proverb that you can grow a tree in ten years but it takes a century to produce a new generation. Twenty years has seen the emergence of a new force: a whole generation of scientists and technicians, who have come into existence in a way that would have been impossible in America or Russia. A young people, with faith in their own future, and in the value of their ideals, will respond willingly to the call of their leaders. This is one important factor, but there is another: the totalitarian nature of the country, which makes it possible to make people concentrate on a definite purpose, using all the human and financial resources they possess, even to the relative detriment of their standard of living.

A third factor has been the importing (from Japan and West Germany, for instance) of the most varied equipment and supplies: precision instruments, special kinds of steel, heat resistant alloys, computers for calculating instantaneously rocket and missile trajectories, and so on. Not to mention, of course, the intensive development of research methods that was achieved with the invaluable help of the U.S.S.R., perhaps the most important element of all.

Even when, in 1950, the Institute of Atomic Energy had been

set up in Peking, attached to the Academy of Sciences, the centre for coordinating research, Chinese scientific development was held back by the launching of the Korean war – a 'limited' war in a nuclear age. China was practically under the direct threat of American atomic weapons; and it was to some extent the nuclear threat that forced her to negotiate a settlement. After the July 1953 Armistice, Chinese atomic development entered a new phase. In 1954, Peking ordered all its nationals studying or doing research in the West to return home. Russia then sent technicians to China. In February 1955, with Russian help, a processing plant was established in Sinkiang, by the Tarim river, for the production of fissile materials for nuclear weapons. From the first, China concentrated on uranium to the exclusion of plutonium, thus evincing her clear determination to produce a thermo-nuclear device as soon as possible! On 29 April 1955 there was a Sino-Soviet agreement to establish in Peking an experimental 10 megawatt reactor using heavy water, consuming uranium enriched to 10 per cent. (It was to start functioning on 27 September 1958.) During the course of 1956, while some twenty high-level Chinese specialists went in March to Moscow-Dubna for training, Russia gave China two reactors: one was set up in Ang Ang-chi (in the north-west), the other in Shenyang (formerly Mukden).

After the secret treaty between Moscow and Peking was signed in October 1957, and the beginning of the Chinese twelve-year plan for the development of science and technology at the start of 1958, an Institute for atomic research was set up in Shanghai in February; at the time same a cyclotron, entirely constructed by the Chinese themselves, was also established there. The ideological dispute between Moscow and Peking, which no more destroyed the international Communist movement than the Reformation destroyed the Church, became apparent in 1958, and grew throughout 1959; it immediately led to a reduction of Soviet aid. China was determined to run her atomic course alone. The Peking Atomic Energy Institute set up a number of institutes all over the country. In Peking, a small research reactor, constructed entirely by Chinese, consumed enriched uranium provided by Russia. The Chinese then went on to build a plant for separating isotopes in Lanchow, which as yet produced uranium enriched only to 25 per cent and not 93 per cent. There they had a 300 megawatt reactor (where it would have been possible to produce a 20-kilo-ton A-bomb, using uranium 235, in a month), which got the energy it needed to function from the series of hydroelectric plants installed along the Yellow River. The following year – when the Soviet technicians were withdrawn – was to see the construction of small experimental reactors in Wuhan, as well as in the provinces of Shensi, and Kirin, and at the University of Nankai.

In 1961–2, more powerful reactors were installed in Sian and Chungking. By then China had more than ten reactors, including two using plutonium near Lanchow. Peking was also provided with an Institute of Mechanics, an Institute of Electronics, an Institute of Automation and Remote Control, while in Wuhan an Institute was set up for studying the Physics of the Upper Atmosphere. Meanwhile, a team of Chinese scientists were sent into Sinkiang to make a study of nuclear weapons and launching methods, under the leadership of Professor Chien San-chiang, Director of the Atomic Energy Institute in Peking. At the same time, building was completed on some forty installations for the extraction of plutonium and thorium, and for separating the plutonium from the uranium waste from the reactors. The first Chinese A-bomb exploded on 16 October 1964, followed by a second on 14 May 1965. China was by then in a position to plan for the H-bomb, for she was now producing the uranium needed to make it, and had conducted experiments in the technique of 'implosion' in her A-bombs, which made it possible to cut down their size, and use them as 'triggers' for fusion reaction. But she did not have the production capacity for weapons in the megaton range that would make her a major nuclear power: for this she would have to make up by advanced methods of delivery. It was here that the famous Professor Chien Hsueh-chien came in. But even had they not had this brilliant scientist of their own, the Chinese could have found in American and German scientific reports all the theoretical and practical knowledge they needed to make an intercontinental missile – and to do so at a hundredth of the cost paid by the U.S.A.

Chinese Science: a Paper Atom?

Three hundred and fifty-three scientists from universities and scientific institutes in 43 foreign countries were invited by their Chinese colleagues to Peking in August 1964; Marshal Nieh Jung-chen, overlord of Chinese atomic weaponry, concluded his address of welcome with these words: 'Modern science is no longer the monopoly of Western countries.' And in fact, in twenty years, red China has become, after the U.S. and the U.S.S.R., the third greatest scientific power in the world.

The advance in nuclear equipment, as I have just shown, is enormously revealing: the field of research grows ever wider, and there are now Chinese scientists producing large-scale computers. Just as the first industrial revolution was inaugurated by the invention of the steam engine, the second industrial revolution has been opened by that of the computer. The development of computers (which will probably, between now and 1980, come to absorb some 5 per cent of the G.N.P. of a developed country) is an extraordinary stimulus to scientific research. The Chinese Institute of Automation and Remote Control is working to capacity, and we are told in a study made by the National Science Foundation of the U.S.A. that 'The mathematicians are first-class, and Chinese electronics experts have set on foot an industry whose products are beginning to appear in various East-European countries.' Computers and translating machines are continually in operation in the Institute of Scientific Information in Peking, collecting and analysing scientific and technological publications from the West. The advance of science and technology in red China – of which the nuclear arsenal is one of the most imposing indications – cannot be questioned. Europe does not want to recognize the fact. Yet all the European experts who have visited people's China have observed the scope and variety of China's scientific advance. For instance, the French four-man mission, Charles Sadron (biologist), Jean Cantacuzène and Georges Ourisson (chemists) and Professor Pierre Piganiol (one of those responsible for the organization of scientific research in France), astounded by, among other things, the incredibly advanced electronic devices they saw for measuring the pH of the soil, gave the French on their return some advice which might also be construed as a warning: 'Whatever you do, don't underestimate Chinese science!'

Since the sciences are not narrowly compartmentalized, no advance hoped for in one can be achieved without making use of the advances already accomplished in others. And in China such advances do not concern any individual branch of science or technology, but the most various disciplines. In the study of molecular engineering, for instance, the Chinese have elaborated the Straton theory, which is fundamentally different from the more traditional American quasar theory. There have been considerable advances for instance, in physics (in the sphere of cyclotrons of atomic piles, and that of spectrographs), in chemistry, improved uses of the laser (the synthesizing of insulin and of chlorophyll). Similarly in geology, and in every sector of industrial technology. Also, of course, in biology, medicine and surgery. For instance, Professor Wang Van-li, a specialist in cancer research and radiotherapy in Nanking, has had remarkable success in treating cancer of the ovary with radioactive gold.

The Chinese, on the other hand, know pretty well everything that is being done in the West: every year they spend some 4 million dollars on the purchase of all the scientific and technical literature published in the West, buying it in Great Britain. Most of the medical electronic apparatus made in China – especially that used in open-heart surgery – could easily bear comparison with anything in the West: Professor Wilder Penfield, a Canadian neuro-surgeon, who assisted at an operation of that kind there, has given glowing reports of it. And one need hardly remind the reader that the synthesizing of insulin demands equipment of the most advanced kind.

Though science in China has thus made strides in spheres far removed from that of weaponry, when it comes to the humanities and sociology, on the other hand, almost nothing seems to be happening. How indeed could any communist regime, with its view of society as something almost sacred, accept sociology? In people's China, no basic research in this area is even dreamt of: the 'thoughts' of Mao – the greatest venture in indoctrination in human history – represent the one and only theory. Everyone has to read them; and no one must ever lose sight of the principles they teach, which must become part of his mental furniture, as well as the context within which his own individual effort has its place and meaning. A Westerner may perhaps have a theoretical concept of what this vast venture is, but it is hardly possible for any non-Chinese really to understand. It is specifically Chinese, having certain elements in common with the past. The Chinese have after all a long tradition of receiving thoughts from higher sources: Confucius probably had no thought of creating the 'Chinese man', but he did so, none the less!

Sacrifice to the Nuclear Gods

China is bubbling away, yet Europe tries to ignore the fact. Though political prophets might prognosticate in a variety of ways, they all agreed on one point: there could be no Chinese nuclear explosion before 1970. By considering the development of people's China as they would that of a country with a modern economic infrastructure, none of them saw, or indeed wished to see, what was actually happening, scientifically and industrially, in China. Given her position in the world, China was determined to sacrifice absolutely everything to the gods of nuclear energy. If we want to set a definite date to the beginnings of this policy, we may perhaps pinpoint June 1958, when Kuo Mo-jo, President of the Academy of Sciences, declared to the world: 'China is entering the atomic age.' But in point of fact the nuclear programme goes back long before then.

For at least three years, nuclear collaboration between Russia and China had been growing ever closer, to Peking's advantage. It would not have seemed exaggerated to talk in terms of the two countries ultimately having a shared nuclear programme. Certainly, in April 1955, there was formed a scientific Commission for National Defence, consisting of two hundred Chinese and a dozen Soviet experts. Two years later, in October 1957, two major Chinese scientific delegations visited Russia; and it was no pleasure trip, since a secret treaty was signed in the Kremlin on 15 October 1957, dealing with 'new techniques for

national defence'.* As events were to show yet again, the Kremlin, whoever the individuals in power, never changed its policy
of being ready to sign agreements with everyone, without feeling
bound to put them into effect. If we think back to 1957, the
events of autumn 1956 in Hungary and in Poland had by no
means finished their repercussions; in Russia itself, on 17 June
1957, following a palace revolution, Khrushchev had been
thrown out, but thanks to the speedy intervention of the army
and its boss, Marshal Yukov, Khrushchev returned to power,
and drove out the anti-Party group of Malenkov, Molotov,
Kaganovitch, Chepilov, Savourov and Pervoukhin – a conflict
typical of collegial leadership in a totalitarian regime. Thus, the
major element in whatever commitments the Kremlin may have
at that time made to Peking, was bound to be something
designed to reinforce the relationships within the socialist camp.
Pravda opened its columns (2 November 1957) to Marshal Liu
Po-cheng, speaking in praise of the Kremlin leaders, and warmly
recognizing the value of Russian help in the modernization of the
Chinese People's Army of Liberation. The Chinese scientific
delegates had barely left Moscow when they were succeeded by
a military mission, led by Marshal Peng Teh-huai, accompanied
by Marshal Yeh Chien-ying and the then Chief of the General
Staff, General Su Yu.

In May 1958, the Minister of Foreign Affairs, Marshal Chen
Yi, told some German journalists at a press conference that 'in
the very near future China will produce a prototype A-bomb'.
Three months later, this was confirmed by Marshal Nieh Jung-
chen: 'In the very near future, we must and can develop the
most modern techniques in the sphere of atomic fission and
thermo-nuclear reaction, and succeed in applying them in such

* It was the *People's Daily* in Peking which revealed the existence and
content of this document in these words: '. . . On 20 June 1959, before there
was a question of any treaty banning or partially banning nuclear tests,
Russia unilaterally broke the treaty relating to new techniques for national
defence which she had signed with China on 15 October 1957, and unilaterally
refused to give China a prototype of the A-bomb, or any technical details
about its production.' (*Renmin Ribao*, 15 August 1963.) Moscow neither
confirmed nor denied this, but reproached Peking so violently for 'this
divulging of state secrets' that one can only assume it to be accurate.

fields as the development of nuclear reactors, of rockets, and the conquest of space. . . .' A proud hope indeed, but doomed to disappointment.

The ideological dispute between Peking and Moscow was peculiarly irritating to Khrushchev. In order to avoid having to hold to the treaty of 15 October 1957 (which he may never have intended to do in the first place) he therefore decided to impose in addition right of inspection, and, further, a unified command for all of Asia – an oriental version of the Warsaw pact, in fact, whose conditions were far from being acceptable to the Chinese. Delayed anger over this was expressed in the *People's Daily*: 'In 1958, the Party leadership in the U.S.S.R. made quite unreasonable demands which would have made China totally militarily dependent on the U.S.S.R. Those demands were legitimately and firmly rejected by the Chinese government.' (*Renmin Ribao*, 6 September 1963.) Thus the end of Sino-Soviet nuclear collaboration gradually loomed closer. Liu Shao-chi, President of the Republic, declared in an interview to the Japanese daily, *Tokyo Shimbun* (22 October 1962), that, as far as the Peking Government was concerned, the break was complete by 20 June 1959. China, left to herself, returned to her 'splendid isolation'.

However, the change of direction led to far-ranging changes in the Chinese high command, with the dismissal, on 17 September 1959, of Marshal Peng Teh-huai, the Minister of Defence. Thus the repeal of the secret treaty of October 1957 led to the same situation in Peking as its original signature had created in Moscow – with the dismissal of Marshal Yukov, the Soviet Minister of Defence, on 26 October 1957. Within a few months of these not very friendly exchanges, came the withdrawal of all Soviet aid, followed in the summer of 1960 by the recall of all the Russian personnel in China, thus leaving half-finished numbers of projects which the *People's Daily* described as follows: 'On 17 July 1960, the Soviet authorities suddenly and unilaterally decided completely to withdraw the 1,390 experts then in China to help us in our work. They tore up 343 contracts concerning those experts and the work they were to do, and annulled 257 documents relating to technical and scientific cooperation.

Since then, they have enormously reduced the supplies of complex equipment, and removed key elements in others ...' (*Renmin Ribao*, 4 December 1963.)

For Peking there was to be no going back: China would henceforth herself produce the necessary means (specialists, research centres, economic planning, etc.) to continue her nuclear programme single-handed. Despite the desperate national economic crisis (1959–61), Peking would mobilize all its resources and manpower to produce an atomic weapon as soon as might be, and they achieved their aim on 16 October 1964. For a first attempt it was almost incredible.

Sinkiang: the Nuclear Heart of China

The assistance given by Russia to China was very different from that given by the U.S.A. to her allies through Marshall Aid. Whereas what the Americans primarily gave was credits to buy American products and raw materials, what Russia gave China was technical aid: thousands of Soviet technicians and experts were working all over that vast country, not merely helping to reorganize industries, but also setting up schools for training Chinese engineers and other specialists; they also assisted in municipal administration and did an enormous amount in the spheres of urbanization and public health. In fact, every area of activity in China was given its allotted number of Soviet experts, though nowhere were so many employed as in industry. The whole Chinese press spoke in the most fulsome terms of the Soviet experts, but the Chinese privately spoke of them with reservations such as one would not suspect from reading the naïve descriptions in the papers, nor the dithyrambic commentaries of the official news agency, Hsin-hua. Under cover of what the *Literatournaja Gazeta* described as 'the friendship of two giants' (18 September 1952), the ever-realistic Soviets were closely engaged with Sinkiang and its vast latent resources. It was their wish to turn this Chinese province into the 'Ruhr of Asia' with its threefold wealth – uranium, oil and tungsten. Of the four combined Sino-Soviet firms founded in 1950 and 1951, two were established in Sinkiang. They were part of the result of the agreements signed in Moscow on 28 March 1950 between Vishinsky and the Chinese ambassador to Russia: the first to materialize was a combined firm for the drilling and processing of oil. The four firms were handed wholly over to Peking on 1 January 1955 (in fulfilment of one of the seven agreements signed on 12 October 1954 between Khrushchev and Chou En-lai in Peking, the texts of which were published in *Pravda* that same day). From then on, the production of uranium was entirely in Chinese hands; thus, since the Middle Empire had given way to the Communist regime, the centre of gravity had moved: Sinkiang, which used to be the back of beyond, is the heart of the China of today and the future. Unlike Xenophon and his search for the sea, Mao's movement has been to the interior, to the least-known parts of the country.

Geographically closer to Soviet central Asia than to red China, Sinkiang, also known as Chinese Turkestan, extends over some 1,600,000 square kilometres of north-eastern China (one-sixth of the whole country), and has about 10 million inhabitants (as against 4 million in 1953). To the 4 million native Uighurs – of Turkish descent – roughly the same number of Chinese have been added.

European headlines will one day be as familiar with the names of this oasis of central Asia as they now are with the famous names of Manchuria. Sinkiang is the autonomous region of the Uighurs (though in this case 'autonomous' indicates not so much relative independence of Peking, as the special nature of its programme of socialist planning, actually more 'progressive' in some ways than elsewhere in China); its capital is Urumchi, and it is clearly bounded by natural frontiers. The area between the Tien Shan (or Heavenly Mountains) and the Kunlun Mountains is the most total desert land in all China (the desert of Takla Makan), and also contains the largest depression in the world, the Tarim basin (900,000 square kilometres) and the deepest one, Turfan (283 metres below sea level).

It is a ghastly desert, leading away from the gem of Lop Nor (some 2,500 square kilometres, though it was six times larger in the pleistocene age), a grey, flat, deadly plain, of hard clay and caked salt, where clouds and rain are almost unknown (20 days, or 50 millimetres rainfall per year), and where China carries out her atomic tests. It is also a real desert in the sense that the capital, Urumchi, is 500 kilometres by air and 800 by roads which must cross 9,000-foot mountains. The next nearest town of any size, Yumen (Gate of Jade), 700 kilometres by air, 800 by land, is one of modern China's main oil centres. Yumen and Urumchi are on the same railway from Lanchow, which has a strategic road running alongside it: the network links up with the railways in Tibet. It was to have been continued – had not the Sino-Soviet dispute prevented it – to become the China–U.S.S.R. Trans-Asiatic Railway. Sinkiang is in fact the western gate, since it gives direct access to Afghanistan, to Kashmir, to Pakistan and to Russia.

Sinkiang, so enormously valuable to Peking economically and strategically, and filled as it is with scientific activity, has been barred to foreigners since 1960. But the United States keeps the area under constant surveillance; following the famous U-2 spy planes, the Americans went on to launch spy satellites: S.A.M.O.S. (Satellite and Missile Observation System), on 3 January 1961, and on 12 July, an improved version: M.I.D.A.S. (Missile Defence Alarm System). On 6 August 1968 the 'Spook Bird' was launched, the first of a highly advanced series. All these have taken it in turn to keep Sinkiang under continual observation, taking photographs in all weathers, day and night. It is now twenty years since Peking began the intensive development of the province's mineral resources, and farming land. The change this wrought in their way of life caused the local population to rebel in 1958 and again in 1962 – rebellions stamped out mercilessly by General Wang En-mao, Military Governor of the Province since 1956, and a member of the National Council for Defence in Peking. The civil Governor, an Uighur, Saifudin, a member of the Central Committee of the Chinese Communist Party, presented the minority groups with the alternative of submitting, or disappearing (either by force or by being exiled to Russia). From then on, no local group was to be permitted any attempt at political subversion or military activity.

With the help of army units, and the manpower provided by the 'reactionaries' sentenced to forced labour to 'reform their ideology', enormous things have been done in a very short time: thousands of hectares of desert land have been transformed into fertile fields. Wherever land has been reclaimed (as in Manass in the north) huge mechanized State farms have been established. Half of the cultivated ground is taken up by wheat; cotton is also grown on a large scale, and there are ultra-modern cotton mills now in Urumchi, Kashgar (5,000 kilometres west of Peking!), and Khotan. Alongside the systematic reclaiming and cultivation of the ground, there is also intensive exploitation of what lies beneath it. For in fact, quite apart from its strategic value, Sinkiang contains a fantastic wealth of minerals, which are being actively and methodically prospected; this work was first begun by the Soviets, who supported their prospecting by building road and rail networks. Certainly, without Russia's aid, both technical and material, there could never have been the amazing development of the sub-soil of Sinkiang that is now taking place – involving copper, manganese, zinc, lead, wolfram, iron, molybdenum, tungsten, gypsum, rock salt, jasper, coal, monazite (known for its high thorium content – an element which can by irradiation be converted into uranium 233 which, like uranium 235, can be used as fuel for nuclear energy). And there is of course petroleum (the estimated resources are 840 million tons), which is to be found for several hundred kilometres along the north slopes of the Tien Shan Mountains, and also between Boukour and Vensu in the south, along the Urumchi–Lanchow railway, which makes this 'China's Baku'. The largest oil centre is Karamai. The deposits there are the richest in China (even richer than those in Yumen in Kansu), and have the further advantage of being usable at once. Around all these deposits they have established the most varied and modern industries; today the major industrial centres are Urumchi, Yining and Kashgar. Sinkiang, with all this intensive development has changed more in the last ten years than in the previous thirty centuries.

And over all, the atom rules. The Chinese nuclear explosions told the world that Sinkiang was the site of tremendous activity. An Institute of Atomic Energy, an offshoot of the Peking Academy of Sciences, has been set up in Urumchi. Uranium, the main deposits of which lie in the border area most directly accessible to Russia (the Soviets played a large part in discovering and developing them, and know more about them than anyone), is being worked by over 400,000 labourers, while something like 100,000 troops stand guard over the numbers of installations which stand camouflaged in the caves of the Ala Shan plateau.

The uranium is processed in the plant for separation of isotopes in Lanchow, the atomic capital of China, which draws its energy from a fantastic hydro-electric scheme on the Yellow River, west of the town.

Sinkiang also possesses a second plant, complementary to the Lanchow one, housing two separation units – one by centrifuge, the other by electro-magnetic separation. This requires a vast quantity of electricity, which is supplied by two gigantic barrages on the Amur river (one centre providing 850 million kW, upstream from Zala, and another yielding 120 million kW, downstream from Amazar).

The Chinese plants for separation of isotopes depend – like the English one – on techniques similar to those used in the U.S.A. Obviously the twelve uranium extraction sites and the nine pre-enrichment processing centres are not all in Sinkiang.

The test site for bombs and rockets at Lop Nor in the Takla Makan desert will also be used for the trials of intercontinental missiles – planned to take place in 1970 at the latest. There is an I.R.B.M. base near Chiu-chiang, where the Chinese test their 800- to 1,000-kilometre range missiles. Another is being completed in Tibet, in the Nagchu Dzong area north of Lhasa – in a good position to threaten the whole of south-east Asia, and parts of Russia.

Nuclear Fireworks

The best-informed European experts, whose predictions of China's possibilities have invariably been proved wrong (whereas American scientists have always had a more realistic view of the facts), were quite convinced that the Chinese would find it incredibly difficult to achieve the advance necessary to make a simple plutonium bomb. The fantastic nuclear firework display which the Chinese were to show the world between 16 October 1964 and 27 December 1968 has led them to have a more realistic attitude towards the Chinese nuclear challenge.

Thus it was on 16 October 1964 that the first 20-kilo-ton Chinese A-bomb was exploded on top of a metal tower on the Lop Nor site. The stupefaction of the European scientists was increased on reading the communiqué issued by the American Atomic Energy Commission, after an analysis of material picked up by specially equipped planes actually inside the radioactive clouds of the explosion. Among other things, it stated on 21 October 1964: 'Additional information concerning the nuclear test made by Communist China on 16 October indicates that what was used was a fissile device using uranium 235. . . .' And, furthermore, it was a highly complex device; for their very first attempt, the Chinese produced a nuclear explosion by means of implosion of fissile matter. Now using uranium does not demand so elaborate a technique as implosion; therefore, leaving aside the French plutonium bombs, the Chinese started off by achieving a result which had been produced by techniques known in only the most developed countries. Coloured peoples all over the world were lost in admiration. Even Formosa trembled with pride – to be Chinese is far more important than to be anti-Communist! For the Chinese that day was a step along the road Peking had chosen to make China a great world power and ultimately triumph over the U.S.A. That first A-bomb was no mere propaganda move, but the first of a series of tests leading to the possession of a full military arsenal.

Further tests then followed, at ever shorter intervals. On 14 May 1965 came another A-bomb, also enriched uranium, of 30 kilo-tons, but this time dropped from a plane and therefore operational. The Atomic Energy Commission stressed in their communiqué that 'the device which exploded on 14 May used uranium 235, and was somewhat more powerful than the first bomb'. And the American physicist, Ralph Lapp, added: 'This fact confirms that the Chinese have a working diffusion plant.' Europeans, however, obstinately continued to look upon the Chinese bombs as the work of clumsy amateurs, far too rudimentary to be reduced in size for transportation by planes or rockets: all too soon they were again to be proved wrong. The Americans, on the other hand – and the Soviets too – were far more aware of the Chinese potential. For instance, in an interview published in the *Seattle Journal* on 28 October 1965, Senator Henry Jackson, an atomic expert in the American Congress, and President of the sub-Committee on Atomic Weapons, declared his conviction that red China would explode her first H-bomb in under two years (in fact it was twenty months: 17 June 1967), and would have intercontinental ballistic missiles by about 1975. And Robert McNamara, the then Secretary of Defence, told a N.A.T.O. council meeting in Paris on 15 December 1965 that China would, by 1967, be in a position to equip her armed forces with intermediate range nuclear-powered rockets (in effect the first test took place just before then, on 27 October 1966), and that in ten years' time she would have intercontinental ones. Given their speed in technological advance, with every test resulting in something new and often quite spectacular, one may come to wonder whether the Chinese will not manage to discover a few scientific and technological 'short-cuts', and thus get there faster than the Americans expect.

The third test was on 9 May 1966: On that day, from a plane, the Chinese exploded a 'doped' A-bomb (a term used by technologists to describe an A-bomb whose energy has been increased by the addition of light elements capable of undergoing a process of fusion, in order to make the bomb more powerful). A White House spokesman stated on 12 May: 'Our analysis makes it appear reasonable to estimate a figure of 130 kilo-tons.' So, Peking, not satisfied with a simple A-bomb, declared its intention of progressing to more powerful devices, even including the terrifying H-bomb.* It then became apparent that

* Atomic fission bombs (powered by the fission of heavy atoms: uranium 235, plutonium 239) can be no more than 100 kilo-tons in power. Hydrogen fusion bombs (with the addition of light atoms – either heavy hydrogen or deuterium, ultra-heavy hydrogen or tritium, or lithium, uniting to form kernels of helium) have tremendous energy. An H-bomb consists of an A-bomb (which starts the fusion reaction of the H-bomb) and a fusible mixture (placed round the A-bomb).

Chinese scientists were pursuing two programmes, each stage in which marked a clear advance over the previous one. The first centred upon the making of atomic bombs; the second was concerned with achieving more powerful devices.

Peking soon realized that while atomic weapons are necessary to a nuclear force, the vehicles to transport them are equally so. Thus, the same super-priority was given to the development of nuclear warheads and methods of delivery, far more complicated than making A- or H-bombs. Shortly before the end of the Sino-Soviet honeymoon, *Pravda* revealed (18 May 1958) that the Chinese were studying Soviet techniques so as to be able to launch their own satellites, and were also working on the construction of rockets. In this, though he did not keep his promise about the 'bomb', Khrushchev was generous (as he informed Averell Harriman in July 1959); rockets were delivered to the Chinese from Autumn 1958, as part of the military aid being given to modernize the People's Army. However, the Kremlin were as disagreeably surprised as anyone else when, on 27 October 1966, the fourth Chinese nuclear test took place, a test this time concerned not with a new bomb, but with the delivery method. What was done was to use an A-bomb of only 20 kilotons, but to explode it in the nose of a missile which, after 700 kilometres of ballistic flight, hit its target, with the accuracy needed to avoid disaster. This meant precision and certainty: miniaturization had therefore been achieved, and furthermore, they clearly had on the ground all the guidance systems needed to ensure the launching of long-range missiles in the future. This particular test was indeed quite unprecedented, since this was the first time anyone had simultaneously tested a rocket and the bomb it was to carry: precisely such a combination as would be used in a war. (The U.S.A. and Russia had never carried out such a test, except possibly to study the effects of atomic explosions at very high altitudes.) With this ground-to-ground missile carrying a nuclear warhead, China proved that she had mastered the technical and industrial problems involved in solving the problem of delivery – which France has still not succeeded in doing! There is clearly still a long way to go before they have rockets which can fly 10,000 or more kilometres and land a charge of several megatons on a precise target; but it is worth remembering that the Chinese, in a single year (which chanced also to be the year when the Cultural Revolution made its public appearance) produced nuclear charges capable of surviving the most rigorous environmental conditions involved in rocket-flight (shocks, vibration, acceleration, etc.). Since they are now obviously satisfactory for operational use, they could at any time be directed against America's peripheral bases in Asia. Furthermore, Soviet Asia and southern Siberia – especially the Russian space bases of Baikonour and Tiouratam – are within Peking's range of fire. Thus the first Chinese device launched on 27 October 1966, showed not only what China could do then, but what she was planning for the future: the achievement of long-range missiles similar to those of America and Russia. Clearly a programme to be reckoned with. 'Since she has a rocket and a nuclear weapon, China's influence will henceforth be irresistible', warned the people's daily (*Renmin Ribao*, 15 November 1966). The Soviets noted the latest Chinese achievement in four brief lines at the bottom of page 5 of *Pravda*. . . . None the less, this gradual erosion of his country's advance over China added to the fears expressed in conversation by the Russian man in the street, despite every appearance of serenity shown by the then occupants of the Kremlin.

On 28 December 1966 came the explosion at a high altitude, and consequent wide dispersal of radioactive material in the upper atmosphere, of a new, 'doped' A-bomb (with enriched uranium 235, uranium 238 and thermonuclear materials) of 100 kilo-tons. There could now be no doubt that the Chinese were on their way to possessing the H-bomb.

Six months later their intense efforts and continuing successes reached their high point; on 17 June 1967 – only thirty-two months after the first A-bomb had exploded – they exploded their first 5 megaton H-bomb. Thus it took the Chinese only two tests to arrive at the megaton range super-bomb – a triumph for science and its theorists. But this H-bomb had yet to become militarily valuable; it must still be miniaturized before it could survive the special conditions it would face in a rocket.

Thus, while the achievement of the A-bomb is relatively –

but only relatively! – easy, the achievement of an H-bomb demands a combination of intense industrial effort and the work of high-level scientists – as all scientists everywhere realize full well. So the speed with which the Chinese managed it was truly fantastic. It took thirty-two months for them to produce their first H-bomb, whereas the U.S.A. took eight years to get from the first A-bomb to a megaton-level H-bomb, Great Britain took five, and Russia four (despite which Tass thought fifteen words quite adequate coverage for the Chinese achievement!). As for France, it took her eight and a half years after her first A-bomb, despite the 500 million francs that went into it, and the 5,000 engineers working at Pierrelat. The nuclear Dragon was growing fast, and for the Chinese people their H-bomb explosion wiped out a hundred years of humiliation by white men.

Countries	First A-bomb	First H-bomb	Time between the two
U.S.A.	16 June 1945	1 November 1952	7 years, 4 months
Great Britain	3 October 1952	17 May 1957	4 years, 8 months
U.S.S.R.	23 September 1949	12 August 1953	3 years, 11 months
China	16 October 1964	17 June 1967	2 years, 8 months
France	13 February 1960	24 August 1968	8 years, 6 months

The test carried out on 24 December 1967, which was, like the earlier ones, recorded by the Atomic Energy Commission, was never reported at all by Peking. Many people at once assumed that it must have been a failure, but it is quite clear that the Chinese atomic scientists could easily have covered up for any failure. As to the facts, there is no doubt: the U.S.A. announced that the bomb had reached a power of about 300 kilotons, and contained thermo-nuclear components (uranium 235 and uranium 238). In other words it was a bomb structurally related to the fission-fusion-fission bombs which release enormous power when they explode. It was a 'dirty' bomb, resulting in a tremendous amount of radioactive fall-out. The fact that the Chinese could, by their fifth test, explode such a bomb meant that they had perfected their mastery of the problems of 'doping'; it also indicated the immense speed with which they were carrying out their research, and further the vast scope of their ambitions. Clearly Peking intended to have the most powerful possible weapons geared to the strategy of war directed against civil populations, thus implying destruction on a massive scale.

As a present for his seventy-fifth birthday, the Chinese atomic scientists gave Mao, on 27 December 1968, an eighth nuclear explosion. A communiqué from Washington stated: 'The American Atomic Energy Commission today announces the detection of a nuclear test in the atmosphere by Communist China, which took place in the Lop Nor area, at about 7.30 a.m. G.M.T. This is the eighth nuclear test in the atmosphere detected by the U.S.A. The explosion had a force of about three megatons, which is more or less the same as that of the sixth Chinese test which took place on 17 June 1967.' Thus the eight Chinese tests between 16 October 1964 and 27 December 1968 were on an ascending scale which indicated rapid progress, and an advanced degree of militarization in the devices tested. Thus, far more significant than the capacity for regular production of highly enriched uranium, were the rigorous scientific and technical preparations for these tests, all conducted with complete success, and thus susceptible of immediate exploitation politically. In the past, we used to like saying that the Japanese could only imitate what had already been done in the West: their Nobel prizes have perhaps modified our arrogance. But the astonishment that some people feel now over the awakening of China is perhaps reminiscent of what our great-grandfathers felt over the Meiji in Japan. . . . Far from being set back by the upheavals of the Cultural Revolution, both scientific efficiency and industrial productivity continued to leap ahead, at least when it came to nuclear achievement. No one could be sceptical any longer. Anxious though we may be, we can at least draw one lesson from what has happened: that there can be political and social situations which inevitably lead to underdevelopment, maintain a slow rate of growth and foster corruption.

The Nuclear Temptation

To minimize the importance of atomic weapons is in line with the positions Mao has adopted in the past: 'Can atomic bombs determine the course of wars? No, they cannot. ... Without individual struggles, by the people, atomic bombs count for nothing.' (*Selected Works*, vol. IV, pp. 21–2.) And to show more clearly still that the atomic bomb need not frighten us so much, the Chinese would send great numbers of people – teams of scientists and military units – into the famous 'death circle' near the explosion area very shortly after a bomb had gone off. But, though it is difficult, it is not impossible to envisage Mao transformed into an Angel of Death: the new problems posed by having nuclear weapons made great changes in Russia, and there is no reason why the same thing should not happen in China.

However, the rulers in Peking are well aware that though China has little to fear from a conventional war (the American Senate has constantly recalled MacArthur's forceful statement that 'Anyone who wants to send American ground troops to fight on Chinese soil needs to have his head examined'), she could still suffer disastrously from long-range weapons. Chou En-lai in fact said as much, at a press conference, during his visit to Somalia in 1964: 'If there were to be an atomic war, China would lose more people than any other country.' (France-Presse Agency, 3 February 1964.)

Though the U.S.A. may be disturbed by the political and military uses to which the Chinese might be tempted to put their nuclear delivery system – now or in the future – people's China, simply because of her geographical position, is very much afraid of the foreign land, sea and air forces based all along her borders – 25,000 kilometres of open frontier! The Chinese Communist leaders are profoundly chauvinistic, and look back nostalgically to the ancient past when the Middle Empire, with its incomparable wealth and civilization, dominated all of Asia. This does not mean that they are anxious to rush boldly into invading anyone, or to play nuclear poker games: patience has always been a strong characteristic of Chinese diplomacy. And in Peking's scale of objectives, the highest place is still given to the determination to preserve its own territory at all cost. But, apart from preserving their control over that, the Chinese leaders are clearly interested – hardly surprisingly – in having on their borders friendly, or at least neutral nations, i.e., nations which will not have American bases on their soil. The Peking regime, in its twenty years of power, has only used armed force twice: the first occasion was the conquest of Tibet, and its restoration to China; the second was the intervention in the Korean war, which the Chinese had not themselves instigated, but which, by being next door to the industrial areas of Manchuria, was a potential threat. (The 1962 attack on the Sino–Indian border stopped as soon as the Chinese troops considered they had inflicted sufficient humiliation on the Indian forces.)

Thus, though publicly making clear their mastery of nuclear science and the technology of weaponry, the Chinese leaders are undoubtedly well aware that twenty or thirty nuclear warheads, an annual production capacity of twelve bombs and, to carry them, rockets with a range of 1,000 kilometres, can hardly be said to make Peking a major military power. They remain determined to follow the road of Mao, even after Mao himself 'has seen God' (the expression he himself used when speaking of his death in an interview with Edgar Snow on 9 January 1965), in order to preserve a certain tension inside the country (with one, two, or more cultural revolutions, and the self-sacrifice of another generation to bring the regime to its fiftieth anniversary), so that China does not stand still.

The size of the problems they still have to face is beyond anything we have ever dreamt of: the colonization of the border provinces (Inner Mongolia, Sinkiang, Tibet) by forced migrations and the Sinization of the local minorities; the development of the necessary infrastructures (communications, industry, etc.); the systematic exploitation of vast agricultural and mineral resources; the control of population development; and the ideological and political control of their whole empire. Obviously such tremendous objectives can only be achieved by the most implacable determination and a strong use of power.

As things are, apart from some such unforeseen disaster as

the preventive destruction of all China's nuclear installations by the U.S.A., nothing can stop China from becoming, sooner or later, a fully nuclear power. Nor can anything stop her from using that power to influence (for good or ill) the international totality of which she is part.

China's emergence as the only native nuclear power in the Far East relates more, at least for the immediate future, to defensive purposes than to any specific plans for expansion through the use of nuclear force; but, in the more distant future, Peking's nuclear capability will force a number of Asian nations to come to a political understanding, a *modus vivendi* of some kind, with their turbulent neighbour, for they will all have to consider whether, ultimately, the U.S.A. would risk the deaths, on the first or second strike, of millions of Americans in defence of Burma, Japan, Thailand, or anywhere else. As Albert Sorel once said: 'There will always be conflict between those who think they can adapt the world to their policy, and those who adapt their policy to the realities of the world.'

Twenty years after the coming of Mao, people's China is now, *mutatis mutandis*, in the same situation which Russia was in under Stalin in 1949: that of a power based on enormous numbers of conventional troops, depending on a 'local' monopoly of nuclear weapons.

People's China has already 'made an appointment' for the day when she will present a genuine danger, and the two Superpowers will be forced to negotiate with her for a new world balance of power.

Red China is no longer just a symbol or an example, but is beginning to create the first problem of the international power structures – already in the making – of the twenty-first century.

BRIEF BIBLIOGRAPHY

The list of works given here makes no claim to be a critical bibliography. Being brief, it cannot be exhaustive. Thus the reader will find mentioned other works which may satisfy his curiosity on various details touched on in this book, and in them he will discover bibliographies of a more complete kind.

I

ABEGG, Lily: *De l'Empire du Milieu à Mao Tse-tung*, Rencontre, 1969

AIRD, John S.: *The Size, Composition and Growth of the Population of Mainland China*, U.S. Government Printing Office, Washington, 1961

BUCHANAN, Keith: *The Chinese People and the Chinese Earth*, G. Bell & Sons, London, 1966

CHESNEAUX, Jean: *L'Asie orientale aux XIXe et XXe siècles*, Presses Universitaires de France (Nouvelle Clio, 1967)

DURAND, John J.: *Communication au deuxième Congrès mondial de la Population*, Belgrade, 20 August–10 September 1965

ÉTIENNE, Gilbert: *La Voie chinoise*, Tiers Monde, Presses Universitaires de France

GINSBURGH, Victor: *La République populaire de Chine: cadres institutionels et réalisations*, vol. II, Brussels, 1963

GOUROU, Pierre: *L'Homme et la terre en Extrême-Orient*, Armand Colin; *L'Asie*, Hachette, 1953

GRANET, Marcel: *La Civilisation chinoise*, Albin Michel, 1968; *Études sociologiques sur la Chine*, Albin Michel, 1953

GROUSSET, René: *Histoire de la Chine*, Fayard

GULIK, R. H. van: *Sexual Life in Ancient China*, Leiden, 1961

GUILLAIN, Robert: *Six cents millions de Chinois*, Julliard, 1956

GUILLERMAZ, Jacques: *La Chine populaire*, Presses Universitaires de France, 1964

JERONIM, Ulrich: *Die fremden Minderheiten im wirtschaftlichen Entwicklungsprozess*, Das Beispiel, Überseechinesen in Sudöstasien Wirtschaftsdienst, July 1966

Law of Marriage in the People's Republic of China, followed by three additions:
    'A Law which Corresponds Closely to our Needs', by Tshang

Tshe-jang, President of the People's Supreme Court (Report on the law of marriage in the People's Republic of China)

'Chinese women in conflict with the feudal system of marriage', by Mme Teng Ying-chao (Mme Chou En-lai), Vice-President of the National Chinese Federation of Democratic Women; Foreign Language Publications, Peking

LÉVY, Roger: *Trente siècles d'histoire de Chine*, Presses Universitaires de France, 1967

Mouvements migratoires et population urbaine en Chine (1953–1957), G.E.P.E.I. Section Extrême-Orient, Paris, March 1966

ORLEANS, Leo A.: *Professional Manpower and Education in Communist China*, National Science Foundation, 1960

PÉLISSIER, Roger: *De la Révolution chinoise*, Julliard, 1967; *La Chine entre en scène*, Julliard, 1963

Population Growth in Mainland China, Committee on the Economy of China, 1966

SAUVY, Alfred: *Malthus et les deux Mao*, Denoel (1963 and 1966); *La Population*, Presses Universitaires de France, 1968; *La Prévention des naissances*, Presses Universitaires de France, 1967

UNITED NATIONS: *World Population Conference, 1965*, vol. II, pp. 29–33, 'The Present and Future Demographic Situation in China', by Roland Pressat

WAUTERS, Arthur, and others: *Le Régime et les institutions de la République populaire de Chine*, Brussels, 1959

2

An Economic Profile of Mainland China, Congress of the United States, Washington, February 1967

BETTELHEIM, Charles: *La Construction du socialisme en Chine*, Diplomatic and Consular Archives, Geneva, 1965

BETTELHEIM, Charles, CHARRIERE, J., MARCHISIO, H.: *La Construction du socialisme en Chine*, Maspero, Paris, 1968

Die wirtschaftliche Entwicklung der Volksrepublik China, A. Metzner Verlag, 1959

Dix glorieuses années (1949–1959), Foreign Language Publications, Peking 1960

DUMONT, René: *Révolution dans les campagnes chinoises*, Paris, 1957; *Chine surpeuplée, Tiers Monde affamé*, Paris 1965.

EBERHARD, W.: *Histoire de la Chine*, Paris 1952

Economic Development of Communist China, University of California Press, 1962

ECKSTEIN, Alexander: *Communist China's Economic Growth and Foreign Trade*, Ann Arbor, 1966

ESCARRA, Jean: *La Chine, passé et présent*, Paris, 1949
Food and Agriculture in Communist China, New York 1966

GOUROU, Pierre: *L'Asie*, Paris, 1953

GROUSSET, R.,: *Histoire de la Chine*, Paris, 1942

GUILLERMAZ, J.: *La Chine populaire*, Paris, Presses Universitaires de France, 1964

ISHIKAWA, Shigeru: *Long-term Prospects for the Chinese Economy*, 3 vols., 1964–1967, Institute of Asian Economic Affairs, Tokyo

JAMINE, V. A.: *Selskoe khozyaistvo Kitaja*, Moscow, 1959

La Transformation socialiste de l'économie nationale en Chine, Foreign Language Publications, Peking, 1966

LI CHOH-MING: *Industrial Development in Communist China*, Praeger, New York, 1964

MENGUY, Marc: *L'économie de la Chine populaire*, Paris, 1965

PERKINS, Dwight H.: *Six Centuries of Agricultural Development in China (1368–1967)*, Aldine Press, 1968

Premier Plan quinquennal de développement de l'économie de la République populaire de Chine, 1953–1957, Foreign Language Publications, Peking

SNOW, E.: *Red China Today*, London, 1970

The Economic Potential of Communist China, Stanford Research Institute, Menlo Park, California, vol. III, May 1964

WALTER, Kenneth R.: *Planning in Chinese Agriculture*, London, 1965

WANG KIUN-HENG: *Précis de géographie de Chine*, Foreign Language Publications, Peking, 1959

WU, U. L.: *Economic Development and the Use of Energy Resources in Communist China*, Praeger, New York, 1963

3

Economic Aid from the Sino-Soviet countries to the underdeveloped countries, O.E.C.D., 1965

Economic Commission for Asia and the Far East, U.N.O., Annual reports

HAMRELL, S. and WIDSTRAND, C.: *The Soviet Bloc, China and Africa*, The Scandinavian Institute of African Studies, Uppsala, 1964

KURDIUKOV, I. F., NIKIFOROV, V. N., PEREVERTAILO, A. S.: *Sovietskokitaiskie otnosbeniia 1917–1957*, Sbornik dokumentov, Moscow, 1959

MAO TSE-TUNG, *Problems of War and Strategy*, 1960; *The People's Democratic Dictatorship*, Peking, 1963

MIYASHITA, Tadao: *Chugoku no bokei soshiki*, Tokyo, 1961

PRYOR, Frederick, L.: *Communist Foreign Trade*, London, 1963

REMER, C. F.: *Three Essays on the International Economics of Communist China*, University of Michigan, 1959

ROSTOW, W. W.: *Prospects for Communist China*, New York, 1954.

SLADKOVSKII, M. I.: *Ocherki ekonomitcheskikh otnoshenii S.S.S.R., Kitaem*, Moscow, 1957

White Paper on trade between Japan and Communist China, Tokyo, 1958

YONEZAWA, Hideo: *Chugoku no Keizai hatten to taigai boeki*, Tokyo, 1964

4

FITZGERALD, C. P.: *The Chinese View of their Place in the World*, Oxford University Press, 1967

GITTINGS, John: *The Role of the Chinese Army*, Oxford University Press, 1967

GUILLERMAZ, Jacques: *Histoire du parti communiste chinois*, vol. I, Payot, Paris, 1968

HO LUNG (Marshal): *The democratic tradition of the people's army of liberation in China*, Peking, 1965, Foreign Language Publications

HSIAO HUA (General, Director of the general political department of the People's Army of Liberation): *Report to the Conference on political work in the Army, January 1966*, Peking, 1966, Foreign Language Publications

JOFFE, Ellis: *Party and Army: Professionalism and Political Control in the Chinese Officer Corps 1949–1964* (Harvard East Asian Monographs, 19), Cambridge, Mass., 1965

LIN PIAO (Marshal): *Long Live the Glorious People's War!*, Peking, 1965, Foreign Language Publications.

LI TSOUO-PENG: *Un contre dix sur le plan stratégique, dix contre un sur le plan tactique*, Peking, 1966, Foreign Language Publications

MAO TSE-TUNG: *Selected Works*, 4 vols., Peking, 1968; *Military Writings* (29 texts); *Quotations from President Mao Tse-tung*, 1st ed. 1966; Foreign Language Publications.

MARTINOV, A. A.: *Literatura o narodno-osvoboditelnoi armii Kitaia*, Moscow, 1957, Voennoe izdatelstvo Ministerstva Oborony Soiuza S.S.R.

PÉLISSIER, Roger: *De la Révolution chinoise*, Julliard, Paris, 1967

Principal Documents on the First Session of the Third National Assembly of the People's Republic of China, Peking, 1965, Foreign Language Publications

Reply of Deputy Prime Minister Chen Yi to some journalists, Peking, 1966, Foreign Language Publications

The Chinese Red Army, 1927–1963 (in preparation at the East Asian Research Center of Harvard University)

WANG LI, KIA YI-HSIUE, LI SIN: *The Dictatorship of the Proletariat and the Great Proletarian Cultural Revolution*, Peking, 1967, Foreign Language Publications

5

BARNETT, A. and VOGEL, E.: *Cadres, Bureaucracy and Political Power in Communist China*, Columbia University Press, New York, 1967

CHENG CHU-YUAN: *Scientific and Engineering Manpower in Communist China 1949–1963*, National Science Foundation, Washington, 1965

DEVILLERS, Philippe: *Ce que Mao a vraiment dit*, Stock, Paris, 1968

DRAPER, Theodore: *Abuse of Power*. The Viking Press, New York, 1967

FONTAINE, André: *Histoire de la guerre froide*, vol. II, Fayard, Paris, 1967

HALPERIN, M. H.: *China and the Bomb*, Praeger, New York, 1965

HSIEH, A. L.: *Communist China's Strategy in the Nuclear Era*, Prentice Hall, 1962; *Communist China and Nuclear Force*, 1963

ICKLE, F. C.: *The Growth of China's Scientific and Technical Manpower*, 1957

Impact of Chinese Communist Nuclear Weapons Progress on U.S. National Security. Report of the Joint Committee on Atomic Energy, July 1967 (our technological information on the Chinese nuclear tests come from this document)

KLOCHKO, M. A.: *Soviet Scientist in China*, International Publishers' Representatives, Toronto, 1963

Nuclear Research and Technology in Communist China, U.S. State Department, Bureau of Intelligence and Research External Research Staff, Washington 1963

(American) White Paper on Sino-American relations, 1844–1949

WHITING, A. S.: *China Crosses the Yalu: the Decision to Enter the Korean War*, the Macmillan Co., 1960

Newspapers and Periodicals

If one keeps abreast of specialist publications, and the newspapers and periodicals which give regular space to Asian affairs, one can follow closely the development of events and ideas there.

Ajia Keizai, no. 12, vol. VII, December 1967, Tokyo

Articles et Documents (52 issues per year), La Documentation française, Paris

Berichte und Informationen (Vienna)

Borba (Belgrade)

Bulletin of the Atomic Scientists, Educational Foundation for Nuclear Science, Chicago

Chugoku Keizi Kenkyu Geppo (JETRO), Tokyo

Das Parlament (Bonn)

Far Eastern Economic Review (Hong Kong)

Foreign Trade of the People's Republic of China (Peking)

G.E.P.E.I., section dealing with the Far East (11 studies published in December 1968, Paris)

Guerre et Paix, review of the Institut Français de Polémologie (Paris)

Hong Kong Trade and Industry (Hong Kong)

Japan Quarterly (Tokyo)

Kommunist (Moscow)

La Croix (Paris)

Le Monde (Paris)

Le Monde diplomatique (Paris)

Military Review, (ed. U.S. Army Command and General Staff College, Fort Leavenworth, Kansas)

Notes et Études documentaires (100 issues per year), La Documentation française (Paris)

Pékin Information (Peking)

Pravda (Moscow)

Population (Paris)

Revue de Défense nationale (Paris)

Revue française de science politique (Paris)

Revue militaire générale (Paris)

Stratégie, review of the Institut français d'études stratégiques (Paris)

The Developing Economies, vol. V, no. 1, March 1967 (Tokyo)

Vniechniaia Torgovlia (Moscow)

Voprossy Ekonomiki (Moscow)

Yearbooks of the F.A.O., the F.E.E.R. (Far Eastern Economic Review), the O.E.C.D., and the U.N.O.

Guangming Ribao (Clarity), daily, Peking

Hongqi (The Red Flag), Peking

Hsinhua ('New China' Press Agency), Peking

Jiefangjun Bao (The army daily), Peking

Kexue Tongbao (Bulletin of the Academy of Sciences), Peking

Renmin Ribao (The People's Daily), Peking

Tongzhi Gongzi Tongxin (Bulletin of Statistics) Peking; this ceased publication in 1957

1949

1 October: Foundation of the People's Republic of China, formation of a provisional central government. Power in the hands of the Council of State of the Central Government, with Mao Tse-tung as its president. Chou En-lai appointed President of the Council of State Administration, and Minister of Foreign Affairs. General Chu Teh Commander-in-Chief of the armed forces.

   The Kremlin breaks with Chiang Kai-chek and establishes diplomatic relations with Peking.

10 October: Mao elected President of the National Council of the Consultative Conference of the People. The Council of State declares 1 October a national holiday in the People's Republic.

19 October: The Council of State decides that the central authority should be administered by 1 president, 4 vice-presidents, 32 ministers and 44 assistant-ministers, and appoints people to these posts.

1 November: The Academy of Sciences founded in Peking, and Kuo Mo-jo, historian, poet and dramatist, appointed its president.

15 November: In a telegram to the U.N., Chou En-lai refuses to accept Nationalist China as representing Peking.

29 November: Radio Peking warns the countries on China's borders that if they harbour nationalist troops they must be prepared to take the consequences.

16 December: Mao in Moscow: his first journey outside China. He was to stay in Russia until 15 February.

1950

14 February: A thirty-year treaty of mutual friendship and aid signed between Moscow and Peking, providing that, in case of aggression by Japan or her allies, the two countries will assist each other.

Each undertakes to enter no alliance or bloc directed against the other, not to intervene in the other's internal affairs, and to give the other every economic assistance.

Agreement reached over Dairen and Port Arthur; the Soviets are to evacuate both, and hand over control of the railway upon the conclusion of the peace treaty with Japan or, at latest, in 1952.

An economic agreement between the two countries: the Kremlin to allow China a credit of 300 million dollars on the basis of 35 dollars per ounce of gold for the purchase of goods. China in return to provide various products, especially tea.

Notes exchanged between Moscow and Peking in which both guarantee the independent status of Mongolia.

28 March: Sino-Soviet agreements signed in Moscow for the setting up of two corporations to work the deposits of oil, natural gas and non-ferrous metals in Sinkiang Province; the running of the companies to be shared equally between the two countries.

1 April: Moscow–Peking agreement over the development of Chinese aviation.

11 April: Ratification by both capitals of the 14 February Agreements.

17 April: Adoption of new Chinese legislation on marriage ensuring equality of rights between the sexes.

12 June: Plenum of the Central Committee of the Communist Party; Mao presents a report on the nation's internal and external situation, and recalls that there remain two provinces to be 'liberated': Taiwan (Formosa) and Tibet.

21 June: Opening of a rail service between China and Russia: six and a half days from Manchouli to Moscow.

25 June: Mao announces to the consultative assembly a programme of redistribution of land to take place over three years.

28 June: Mao declares: 'Asian affairs should be handled by Asian peoples and *not* by the U.S.A.'

15 October: Entry into Korea of 'volunteers of the Chinese People' in the guise of the 'Movement to Resist America and Aid Korea'.

27 October: Peking orders its troops to enter Tibet.

28 December: All American goods in China sequestrated.

1951

3 May: Complete reorganization of the whole Chinese customs system.

27 May: Radio Peking announces the signing of a Sino-Tibetan agreement for the 'peaceful liberation of Tibet', which is to

become a Chinese province under a local government. Peking to regulate its foreign affairs and commerce. Chinese troops to remain there.

25 June: Peking approves the Malik proposal for ending the Korean war.

10 July: Opening of the Kaesong Armistice Conference.

7 September: The apostolic nuncio, Mgr Riberi, expelled from China.

1952

6 May: Chou En-lai declares that the separate peace treaty with Japan had been unlawfully forced upon the people of Japan.

15 June: China recognizes the Geneva Conventions in regard to the treatment of prisoners-of-war and the wounded, and the protection of civilians in time of war.

7 November: In a speech marking the 35th anniversary of the October Revolution, Chou En-lai refers to 'the immense material and technical aid' given to China by Russia for the past three years.

24 December: To the consultative assembly, Chou En-lai announces the government's decision to launch, in 1953, a five-year plan of reconstruction and industrialization, which will only be achieved with 'considerable Soviet aid'.

1953

12 January: Announcement of the formation of a Politburo of nine members inside the Chinese Communist Party.

1 March: Mao declares the coming into effect of the electoral law adopted on 22 February, patterned on the Soviet system.

5 March: Death of Stalin.

27 July: Armistice in Korea.

18 September: Elections put off until the end of January.

1954

6–10 February: Plenum of the Central Committee (Mao being absent): posthumous condemnation of Kao Kang, one of the leading party officials, who had committed suicide in Shenyang.

3 March: Peking agrees to take part in the Geneva Conference.

23 March: Mao presides over a meeting of the committee formed to

study the Constitution of the Republic produced by the Party Central Committee.

14 June: The Government adopts the projected Constitution.

28 June: Chou En-lai and Nehru declare five principles for peaceful co-existence.

20 July: Signing of the Peace Treaty with India.

23 August: Solemn proclamation of the Chinese people's determination to liberate Formosa.

20 September: Unanimous adoption of the Chinese Constitution by the National Congress.

21 September: Congress adopts the four basic Laws of the State.

27 September: Congress unanimously elects Mao President of the Republic, and General Chu Teh Vice-President.

28 September: Congress appoints Mao President of the National Defence Council, and names other members of the Government. Chou En-lai is Prime Minister, General Peng Teh-huai, Minister of Defence. Also appoints the ten deputy prime ministers, and the members of the National Defence Council (15 vice-presidents and 80 members).

29 September: Khrushchev and Bulganin in Peking.

1 October: Fifth anniversary of the regime. The army is told: 'The glorious duty of the army is to liberate Formosa.'

31 October: the Bureau of Statistics announces that according to the census of 30 June 1953, the population of China has reached 601,938,035.

21 December: A loan of 6 billion yuan is floated (1 yuan = 17½p).

1955

31 January: The Council of State (i.e. government) hears a report from Chou En-lai on the Soviet proposals for technical and scientific aid in the development of atomic energy.

9 February: Reform of the armed forces; military service made obligatory.

1 March: Fiscal reform, with the new yuan to be worth 1,000 old yuan (this to be completed by 10 June).

7 April: Proclamation of the end of a state of war with Germany.

17–24 April: Afro-Asian Bandung Conference.

6 May: Soviet troops evacuate Port Arthur and Dairen; their establishments were officially handed back to Peking on 24 May.

5–30 July: Session of the National People's Congress, report on the first five-year plan: 88·8 per cent of all investment to go into heavy industry.

22 September: Opening in Peking of the first State department store on the Soviet pattern.

23 September: The ten generals who are vice-presidents on the National Council for the Armed Forces raised to the rank of Marshal.

17 October: Mao announces that agrarian reform has entered a new phase.

1956

4 January: Opening of a line from Peking to Moscow via Mongolia.

17 January: Adoption of the twelve-year plan for reafforestation.

26 January: A new twelve-year plan for agricultural resources.

29 January: Mao appeals to the Communist Party to make up for China's being so behindhand in science and technology.

30 January: The Party considers a twelve-year plan for helping scientists to 'compete with the best of their colleagues all over the world'.

7 February: The consultative political Conference adopts a resolution on the liberation of Formosa – to be peaceful unless force becomes absolutely necessary.

11 February: Nationalization of private commercial and industrial firms.

7 April: Sino-Soviet economic agreement: Russia to help China build 55 industrial installations at a total cost of 2,500 million roubles during the last two years of the first five-year plan.

15–30 June: Session of the National Assembly, and adoption of the budget: 31 thousand million yuan, 20 per cent of which to be devoted to defence spending.

13 September: Reform of the rural cooperatives, and the allowance of small pieces of land to individuals for their personal use, with the gradual establishment of a free market for foodstuffs and manure.

12–27 September: Opening of the Eighth Congress of the Chinese Communist Party on 17 September, Mikoyan paid tribute to 'the eminent Marxist–Leninist Mao Tse-tung'. By the time it closed on 27 September, the Congress had adopted new statutes for the party and elected a new Central Committee (with 97 permanent members as opposed to the 50 there had been before).

10–15 November: Plenum of the Central Committee, at which Mao calls upon Party Members to 'struggle against the pan-Chinese chauvinism being directed against minority nations living on Chinese soil'.

3 December: Annulment of the second five-year plan, and its re-placement by a completely new project.

29 December: *Renmin Ribao* publishes a report put out by the Party's political office on the historical significance of the dictatorship of the proletariat.

1957

27 February: Mao's 'Hundred Flowers' speech, which had been in preparation since 2 May 1956, and was not finally completed until 8 June 1957.

6 March: Lu Ting-yi, head of the propaganda section of the Communist Party, launches a new campaign for 'ideological rectification within the Party'.

7 March: Mme Li Te-tchouan, Minister of Health, declares: 'A birth control programme must be established at once.'

5 May: As part of the campaign of rectification 'to resolve contradic-tions within socialist society', high functionaries, military leaders and intellectuals are in future to be sent to work in factories and farms.

19 May: Publication of regulations on birth control.

18 June: Publication of the speech given by Mao on 27 February to the Supreme State Conference 'On the correct way to deal with the contradictions existing among the rank and file of the people'.

22–24 July: Special session of the Politburo and the Permanent Com-mittee of the Party Central Committee.

8 September: Admission to the Central Committee of 25 'high-ranking' intellectuals.

2–21 October: Mao in Moscow for the second time. On the 6th he addresses an extraordinary meeting of the Supreme Soviet, declar-ing: 'Our fate, indeed our every breath is one with the Soviet Union.'

26 October: Two Chinese scientific delegations go to Moscow.

6–27 October : Chinese Military Mission to Moscow.

7 December: Li Fu-chun gives the first hints about the second five-year plan to the Trades Union Congress: priority to be given to heavy industry, but considerably more attention than in the past to agriculture.

11 December: Publication of a project for the phonetic transcription of Chinese characters into the 26 letters of our alphabet.

1958

1 February: Session of the National Assembly, with the exclusion of 54 deputies, three of them ministers. Chou En-lai resigns from Foreign Affairs, and at his request, is replaced by Marshal Chen Yi.

3 May: The start of the Great Leap Forward.

16 July: The official declaration: 'The 600 million Chinese will give their fullest aid to the struggle of the Arab peoples.'

31 July: Khrushchev secretly leaves for Peking. Tass announced it in a communiqué on 3 August.

3 August: A communiqué published stressing the complete unity of view between the two countries on the problems of the day.

4 August: The Central Bureau of Statistics publishes a report on the results of the Great Leap Forward campaign in industry and agriculture.

29 August: Special session of the Central Committee of the Party in Peithao, approving the establishment of the people's communes.

4 September: Peking officially announces that its territorial waters are to extend for twelve miles. Russia recognizes nine.

12 October: Appointment of General Huang Ke-cheng to the post of Chief of the General Staff in succession to General Su Yu.

25 October: The last Chinese troops leave Korea.

28 November–10 December: Plenum of the Central Committee in Wuhan.

16 December: Marshal Chen Yi, Minister of Foreign Affairs, tells the diplomatic corps: 'The Central Committee of the Communist Party decided in plenary session, on 10 December 1958, to approve President Mao's suggestion not to ask the National Assembly to renew his term as President of the Republic.'

17 December: Official communiqué from the plenum of the Central Committee, announcing Mao's decision to resign as President of the Republic when his four-year term ends in 1959.

1959

27 January: Declaration by Khrushchev: 'There is not and cannot be any divergence between Russia and China. On all points we are in agreement with our brother Communists in China, even though their methods for the building up of socialism may differ from ours on certain points.' The next day Chou En-lai confirmed this statement.

10 March: Publication in the U.S.A. of the secret report given to the Senate two months earlier by John Foster Dulles on the situation in China.

17 March: Uprising in Tibet.

26 March: Meeting in Peking of delegates from the army, navy and air force.

28 March: Dissolution by Peking of the local Tibetan Government. India gives political asylum to the Dalai Lama.

13 April: Publication of the balance sheet of the first five-year plan.

27 April: Election of Liu Shao-chi as President of the Republic by 1,156 votes out of 1,157.

28 April: Formation of Chou En-lai's government, with sixteen vice-presidents of the Council, and thirty-eight ministers and presidents of Commissions.

5 May: Meeting of the Council of Defence elected on 28 April.

15 June: Moscow (secretly) denounces its atomic agreement with Peking.

1 July: The Chinese Government decides to adopt the metric system.

2–16 August: The Central Committee sits in Lashaa (Kiangsi Province) under the chairmanship of Mao. This 8th plenum of the Central Committee condemns Marshal Peng Teh-huai, Minister of Defence, for his opposition to the Party, to the Great Leap Forward and the people's communes. It further accuses him of having supported Kao Kang, the former Governor of Manchuria who had been dismissed in 1954 for having tried to link it too closely with Russia. (Extracts from this resolution were to be published on 15 August 1967 by the official agency Hsinhua.)

29 August: First anniversary of the people's communes: 120 million peasant families – in other words 99 per cent of the people living in the countryside – now living in 24,000 people's communes.

13 September: The permanent committee of the National Assembly approves a report from Chou En-lai about the Sino-Indian border dispute, and the opening of negotiations on the basis of the five principles of peaceful coexistence.

17 September: Ministerial re-shuffle. Marshal Peng Teh-huai dismissed as Minister of Defence, and General Huang Ke-sheng replaced by General Lo Jui-ching, as Chief of the General Staff.

30 September: Arrival of Suslov and Gromyko in Peking.

1 October: Solemn celebration of the regime's tenth anniversary.

6 October: Declaration by Chou En-lai on China's international role.

November: Mao leaves Peking – to return six months later.

4 December: The people's supreme court decides to free Aisin Gioro Pu Yi, aged 50, the last Emperor of China. He became a gardener in the Peking botanical garden, a member of the Communist party and Manchu deputy under the name of Henry Pu Yi; he died in 1967.

21 December: *Renmin Ribao* issued an appeal for a further 'Leap Forward' in 1960, and a 'technological revolution' in order to achieve in three years what had been planned to take five.

1960

7 January: Ministerial re-shuffle; nine new vice-ministers, and the appointment of new diplomats and new rectors of universities.

28 January: Treaty of friendship and non-aggression, and a boundary settlement with Burma.

30 March–10 April: Opening of the annual session of the National Assembly. Li Fu-chun, President of the planning commission, announces that China is three years ahead on the major objectives of her second five-year plan.

16 April: Publication in Peking of an article called 'Long live Leninism', criticizing, though without naming him, the 'revisionism' of Khrushchev.

8 June: Congress of the World Federation of Trades Unions in Peking; first rumblings of the Sino-Soviet dispute.

21 June: During the Rumanian Party Congress, a dispute occurs between Khrushchev and the Chinese delegates.

18 July: Press conference of John F. Kennedy, the new President of the U.S.A., in which he says that any agreement with Russia over atomic tests must be incomplete without the participation of people's China.

22 July: Opening of the 3rd National Congress of Chinese artists and men of letters. From it emerges the fact that there are 2,800 theatres, 3,515 repertory and touring companies, and 260,000 persons working in the arts.

17 August: Article by Li Fu-chun in *Hongqi*: priority must be given to agriculture, and especially to cereal crops. All Russian technicians recalled, and all contracts repudiated.

12 October: Ratification of the Sino-Mongolian friendship and mutual aid treaty signed on 31 May at Ulan Bator.

5 November: The official agency, Hsinhua, publishes a declaration by Sun Yat-sen's widow, Soong Ching-ling, sister-in-law of

Chiang Kai-chek and Vice-President of the Peking Republic, to the effect that the close union between the two giants, China and Russia, will be a decisive factor in determining the course of history.

11–25 November: Conference in Moscow of the 81 Communist Parties of the world.

29 November: Radio Peking reveals that in 1960 Chinese agriculture has suffered one of the worst series of natural disasters of the century.

20 December: The Creation of the N.L.F. in South Vietnam.

Ratification of the Sino–Burmese frontier treaty signed on 1 October.

1961

16–18 January: Meeting of the Central Committee. A communiqué issued recognizing the existence of 'temporary difficulties' in food supplies. The Central Committee decides to reorganize the Party by setting up six bureaux from the Central Committee to do what is most urgently needed in the main areas of the country.

1–10 February: Large-scale purchases of cereals from Australia and Canada.

2 February: The Party decides to intensify its surveillance of establishments of higher education.

5 May: Creation within the Government of a general office for foreign economic relations.

30 June: To mark the fortieth anniversary of the Chinese Communist Party, the President of the Republic launches an appeal to all its peoples to fight against 'the number one enemy, American imperialism'.

2 July: In Geneva, Marshal Chen Yi, Minister of Foreign Affairs, declares: 'China is too heavy to become anyone else's satellite.'

23 July: Ministerial re-shuffle: seventeen appointments to positions in the Government.

31 August: The Peking Government makes a statement approving the Soviet Government's decision to return to nuclear testing: it is 'a means of making those who foment war see reason'.

19 October: Speech in Moscow of Chou En-lai to the 22nd Congress of the Soviet Communist Party. He accuses Khrushchev of having acted in a non-Marxist manner by openly publicizing disputes between brother-parties and brother-nations to the enemy, and ostentatiously leaves the meeting hall. On 21 October, he lays

wreaths on the tombs of Lenin and Stalin, and on the 23rd he leaves for Peking. Tass announced that he had gone to take part in the meeting of the Chinese National Assembly.

7 November: The Chinese leaders are out of Peking for the anniversary of the Soviet Revolution. Peking radio puts out a long and emotional eulogy of Stalin.

1962

27 March–16 April: Opening of the National Assembly session held in private.

30 April: Marshal Chen Yi gives a speech in which he recognizes that it will take years of arduous struggle to turn China into a strong socialist country, but adds that under Mao's leadership it will be achieved.

4 July: Departure for Moscow of a scientific delegation led by Chin Li-cheng and for East Berlin of a scientific and technological delegation led by Hsiao Kueichang.

23 July: Press conference held by Marshal Chen Yi in Geneva: 'Relations between the U.S.A. and China could improve if the U.S.A. would evacuate Formosa.'

3 August: Interview with Marshal Chen Yi broadcast on Italian–Swiss radio: 'The Chinese Government is beginning to arm its forces with nuclear weapons, but it will take some time before we have atomic bombs.'

9 September: A U-2 plane brought down in eastern China.

24–27 September: 10th plenum of the Central Committee. Three new secretaries appointed to the committee: Lu Ting-yi, head of propaganda for the Communist Party, Kang Shen, head of the secret service; and General Lo Jui-ching, Chief of the General Staff.

20 October: Lightning offensive by China in the Himalayas.

31 October: China's admission to the U.N. rejected by 56 votes to 42.

18 December: The permanent Bureau of the Communist Party decides to recall the national Assembly in the second half of 1963. After this session general elections will take place.

1963

6 January: *Hongqi* declares that 'recent history has shown Mao to be right in saying sixteen years ago – in conformity with Leninist teaching – that imperialism is only a paper tiger'.

26 April: Japan grants China a credit of £2,600,000 at 5 per cent to be repaid in eighteen to twenty-four months.

3 May: Beginning of the Cultural Revolution (as quoted by Mao himself in an article in *Renmin Ribao* on 17 July 1966).

4 June: An air-force pilot from Formosa lands in people's China with his American F-86 F aircraft; he is rewarded with 2,500 ounces of gold.

14 June: The Chinese Party denounces Russia (the '25 points').

14 July: Reply by the Russian Party to the Chinese: ideological break between Moscow and Peking.

27 July: Speech by Kuo Mo-jo, President of the Academy of Sciences: 'The time is not far off when China will have mastered the techniques of nuclear weapons.'

13 September: *Renmin Ribao* and *Hongqi* publish a long article, 'On the thought of Stalin' in which Peking recalls Khrushchev's role as Stalin's colleague.

21 September: Moscow deplores China's determination to attain atomic weapons at any cost, and accuses Peking of having violated the Sino-Soviet border more than 5,000 times.

4 October: Foundation of the Sino-Japanese friendship Association in Peking.

11 October: China grants Algeria a long-term, interest-free loan of 50 million dollars.

15–16 November: Meeting of the supreme State Conference.

17–30 November: Session of the National Assembly in camera. A communiqué was put out on 3 December announcing that the Assembly would be reformed in 1964 with more than twice the number of deputies (now 1,226), the better to reflect the life of the country.

12 December: Chou En-lai, the head of government, goes for a tour of Africa together with Marshal Chen Yi, Minister of Foreign Affairs – a tour lasting until 15 March 1964. In the interim, the Secretary-General of the Party, Teng Hsiao-ping, is Acting Prime Minister.

16 December: Death of Marshal Lo Jung-huan, a grand old man of the Party leadership.

1964

4 January: Ten poems by Mao published in the Chinese papers.

23 January: Official Chinese protest over the entry of the 7th American Fleet into the Indian Ocean.

27 January: Simultaneous publication in Peking and Paris of a communiqué announcing the establishment of diplomatic relations between the two countries.

3 March: France supports the admission of China to the U.N.

6 March: Liberation of the last Japanese prisoners-of-war still held in China.

27 April: General Huang Cheng named Chinese ambassador to Paris. He was to present his letters of credence at the Élysée palace on 6 June.

8 May: Peking publishes its secret correspondence with Moscow, and refuses to take part in a World Conference of Communist Parties.

Publication of the first edition (by and for the armed forces) of the Little Red Book of quotations from Mao.

30 June: Warning from Valerian Zorin, Russian Vice-Minister of Foreign Affairs: 'The Soviet Union cannot use its nuclear force to support the specific objectives of China.'

Signing in Ulan Bator of a formula for settling the Sino-Mongolian frontier problems.

Editorial in *Hongqi* entitled: 'A great Cultural Revolution'.

6 July: A warning from Peking: 'China will not sit with its hands folded watching aggression against North Vietnam.'

7 July: A U-2 plane brought down over southern China.

31 August: Closing in Peking of the scientific symposium of four continents.

2 September: *Pravda* denounces China's territorial claims against Russia.

11 September: Mao receives Jacques Duhamel, Bernard de Gaulle and Guillaume Georges-Picot.

12 September: Peng Chen is re-elected Mayor of Peking.

29 September: Washington announces that China's first atomic bomb may be exploded 'in the near future'.

14 October: Demotion of Khrushchev.

16 October: Exploding of the first Chinese A-bomb.

17 October: In a message to heads of governments all over the world, Chou En-lai suggests summoning a world conference to discuss the banning and destruction of all nuclear weapons.

12 December: Publication of the list of the 3,037 deputies elected in September to the Third National Assembly, to serve until the end of December 1968.

21 December: Meeting of the new Assembly. Chou En-lai presents them with a report to be published on 30 December.

1965

3 January: Re-election of Liu Shao-chi as President of the Republic for another four-year term.

13 January: Adjournment of the Afro-Asian Conference that was to have taken place in March. It was later put off to the end of May, then to 25 June, then to 5 November, and finally adjourned *sine die*.

24 January: Chou En-lai proposes the formation of an 'Organization of revolutionary United Nations', after Indonesia's leaving the U.N. on 21 January.

5 February: Kosygin, on his way to Hanoi, stops in Peking, and meets Chou En-lai. On his way back, he meets Mao in Peking, on 11 February.

14 February: Peking claims the right to come to Hanoi's aid, and gives Washington warning of the fact, recalling the precedent set by the Korean war.

25–26 February: Peking and Hanoi refuse all idea of a further Geneva Conference on Vietnam, unless their conditions are accepted first.

1 March: Meeting in Moscow, despite Chinese opposition. Peking launches a great campaign against the 'splinter activities of modern revisionists'.

2 March: Opening of the American attack on North Vietnam.

14 May: Explosion of the second Chinese A-bomb.

7 August: New edition of the quotations from Mao, with a preface by the political department of the army.

1 September: Tibet becomes an autonomous region, the fifth in China.

3 September: Publication of a major article by Marshal Lin Piao: 'Long live the victorious people's war!'

10 September: Meeting of the Central Committee at which Mao makes a strong attack on Liu Shao-chi.

16 September: Peking demands that India dismantle, within three days, its military installations on the Sikkim border.

25 September: In a note to India, Peking repeats its claims to 90,000 square kilometres of Indian territory.

29 September: In the U.N. France speaks in favour of the admission of China.

Marshal Chen Yi states that henceforward China refuses to collaborate with 'moderate revisionists and imperialists'.

30 September: Failure in Indonesia of an attempted coup d'état (directly or indirectly inspired by Peng Chen, Mayor of Peking),

with half a million deaths. The pro-Chinese Indonesian Communist Party banned on 18 October.

8–17 October: The general Assembly of the U.N. rejects the admission of China.

10 November: *Wen Hui Bao*, the Shanghai daily, publishes an article strongly critical of a historical play, *The Destitution of Hai Juei*, by Wu Han, assistant Mayor of Peking: this marked the opening of the attack by Mao and Lin Piao on the leadership of the Communist Party.

26 November: Mao, who had left Peking (not to return until the 10 May 1966 to receive the president of the Albanian Council) receives a Cambodian military mission in Shanghai.

1966

1 January: Start of the third five-year plan, but its objectives not made public.

3–15 January: A three-continent conference held in Havana brings together over 500 delegates from governments or revolutionary movements in Asia, Africa and Latin America. Havana chosen as the provisional centre for the Tri-continental Organization of People's Solidarity.

24 January: Publication in Peking of the report presented by General Hsiao Hua, Director of the political department of the army, to the Conference on Political Work in the Armed Forces.

6 February: A violent diatribe against China by Fidel Castro.

23 March: Peking refuses to send delegates to the Soviet Party Congress.

26 March–19 April: Visit by President Liu Shao-chi and Marshal Chen Yi and their wives to Pakistan, Afghanistan and Burma (from which Liu Shao-chi twice rushed suddenly back to China on 31 March and 8 April).

18 April: The army paper, *Jiefangjun Bao*, officially launches the Cultural Revolution.

9 May: Exploding of the third Chinese A-bomb.

10 May: Back in Peking after six months' absence to greet the Albanian head of Government, Mao departs again, not to return till July.

23 May: Celebration with unusual splendour of the 25th anniversary of Mao's book, *Interventions in the Discussion of Literature and Art in Yenan*.

1 June: Mao approves the first 'big character' poster (*tatsi-pao*) put up at the University of Peking (as reported in *Hongqi*, no. 9,

1967), which marks the opening of the critical phase of the Cultural Revolution, with the Red Guards, and big street demonstrations.

3 June: Reorganization of the Peking Party committee, with Peng Chen, Mayor of Peking, expelled.

16 July: Mao's olympic exploit of swimming fifteen kilometres in the Yang-tse in an hour and five minutes (*Hsinhua* official communiqué, 25 July).

18 July: Mao returns to Peking.

1–12 August–11th plenum of the Party Central committee – only made public officially on 13 August.

5 August: Poster in big characters personally put up by Mao: 'Fire on the headquarters!' (i.e., of the concealed bourgeoisie in the State and within the Party).

8 August: Publication of the sixteen-point Decision on the Great Proletarian Cultural Revolution.

18 August: First appearance of the Red Guards. Mao and Lin Piao present at a gathering of a million Red Guards. There were to be others (15 September, 18 October, 3, 10, 11, 25 and 26 November) attended by between 1 and 2 million young people from all parts of China.

27 October: Fourth Chinese nuclear test: the launching of a rocket guided by remote control, carrying a nuclear warhead.

12 November: Great Meeting in the great hall of the National Assembly for the centenary of Sun Yat-sen. The chief leaders were there, as well as Liu Shao-chi and Teng Hsiao-ping who came late by a concealed door, and whom the Hsinhua agency cameras rather ostentatiously ignored.

23 November: Posters denouncing the President of the Republic and the Secretary-General of the Communist Party (though never by name).

3 December: Upheavals in Macao. On 20 December, the Portuguese authorities agree to the demands made by Peking.

4 December: Arrest of Peng Chen, former Mayor of Peking.

24 December: Arrest of Marshal Peng Teh-huai, former Minister of Defence.

28 December: Fifth Chinese nuclear explosion – a 'doped' bomb.

1967

8 January: A specially splendid celebration of the anniversary of the Tsuni Conference (Province of Kweichow). It was in that small town, on 8 January 1935, that Mao was elected President of the

Revolutionary Committee (in succession to Chou En-lai) and President of the Political Bureau, a newly established post. The era of Mao had begun.

12 January: Reorganization of the committee responsible for the Cultural Revolution in the armed forces, now placed directly under the authority of the military commission of the Party Central Committee, and the Group in that Committee responsible for the Cultural Revolution in general.

25 January: Work begun on a twenty-one kilometre rail-link between Changsha, capital of Hunan province, and Shaoshan, the village where Mao was born.

27 January: Violent incidents in Paris between the local police and Chinese students demonstrating outside the Russian embassy.

28 January: Publication of Mao's study, 'The Elimination of Erroneous Ideas in the Party'. Announcing the Rectification of Left-wing Errors Resulting from the Excessive Enthusiasm and Lack of Maturity of the Red Guards and 'Rebels of the Revolution'.

29 January: Directive of the military commission of the Party Central Committee forbidding arbitrary arrest, and the forcing of 'reactionary elements' to march wearing paper hats. Mao approved this directive.

31 January: Establishment of the first of the revolutionary committees, in Heilungkiang; the two last such committees were set up by 5 September 1968.

4 February: The army takes control of the police and security forces in Peking.

5 February: Creation of a Commune of Shanghai (modelled on the Paris Commune).

24 February: Chou En-lai decides to put a stop to excesses: the army gradually establishes control over public life.

7 March: Re-opening of primary and secondary schools all over China.

16 March: The militia called on to support the regular army.

22 March: The whole industrial sector taken over by the army.

1 April: The Peking papers publish the harshest criticisms of the political record of Liu Shao-chi, the 'Chinese Khrushchev'.

9 April: The military commission of the Central Committee issues a warning (dated 6 April) to the army, blaming it for the excesses which it is its very job to prevent. Mao approves this warning.

16 May: A circular produced by the Central Committee on 16 May 1966 made public, to be described on 18 May as a 'great historic document', heralding further Cultural Revolutions in the future.

8 June: Strict measures for keeping order: a formal ban on violence, arbitrary arrests, requisitioning things from houses or offices, theft and destruction.

11 June: Violent attack against 'French imperialism' in the Peking papers.

17 June: Explosion of the H-bomb.

26 July: The Shanghai daily confirms that the two envoys from Peking, General Hsieh Fu-chih, Minister of Security, and Wang Li, Director of Propaganda for the Communist Party, detained in Wuhan (capital of Hupeh Province) on 21 July.

5 August: The President's self-criticism fails to satisfy Maoists.

15 August: The publication of extracts from the resolution adopted on 16 August 1959, at the 8th plenary session of the Party's Central Committee.

22 August: Red Guards set fire to the British embassy in Peking.

24 September: The Chinese press reveals that Mao has recently made a tour of inspection in the North, the southern Central area and the East of China, and has inquired into the development of the Cultural Revolution in the various provinces.

27 September: Signing in Moscow of a formula for commercial exchanges between China and Russia in 1967 (to be at a slightly lower volume than in 1966).

1 October: Mao and Lin Piao assist at a march-past to mark the 18th anniversary of the setting up of the regime. A new list of the country's leaders published by the official press agency.

9 October: In a speech in Wuhan, Chou En-lai gives a realistic balance-sheet of the Cultural Revolution: 'Economically speaking, China has had to pay dearly for so powerful a revolutionary movement; production has been particularly affected where there have been disturbances.'

9 November: Renewal for only one year of the expiring Sino-Japanese commercial agreement for 110 million dollars (known as the L-T Agreement, which was signed for five years on 9 November 1962).

15 November: Opening, a month late, of the autumn fair in Canton. It closed on December 14, having been visited by 7,000 foreigners, 1,000 of them Japanese.

28 November: Yet again Peking is turned down by the U.N.

24 December: Seventh Chinese nuclear explosion, passed over in total silence by Peking.

1968

8 January: The 134th interview (the first having taken place in 1955) between the ambassadors of China and the U.S.A. in Warsaw.

28 March: Dismissal of General Yang Chen-wu, Chief of the General Staff, of Yu Li-jin, Political Commissar for the Air Force and General Fu Chong-pi, Commandant of the garrison of Peking.

3 April: The Peking daily describes France's financial and monetary offensive against the U.S.A. 'as precipitating the imperialist camp into a further fragmentation'.

15 April: Opening of the spring fair in Canton; it closed on 14 May, after visits from 3,000 foreigners.

10 May: The Paris representative of the Hsinhua official agency returned to China just before the opening of the Paris Vietnam conference.

13 May: Talks between America and North Vietnam open in Paris.

21 May: Vast demonstration in Peking in support of the students' revolt in Paris.

4 June: General Huang Yong-cheng, deputy member of the Party Central Committee and Commandant of the Canton military district appointed Chief of the General Staff.

5 August: In an article entitled: 'Let us Unite under the Leadership of the Proletarian Headquarters Directed by President Mao', *Renmin Ribao* condemns the tendencies to 'polycentrism' which have appeared in the country, and concludes: 'The proletarian headquarters, with President Mao as Commander-in-chief, and Vice-President Lin Piao as assistant Commander-in-chief, is the one and only governing centre of the whole of the Party, of the Armed forces, of the country, and of the revolutionary masses. The Party, the Army and the whole country can have but a single centre; there cannot be a second.'

7 September: All the newspapers publish identical editorials, declaring: 'Long live the total victory of the great Cultural Revolution', and hailing the establishment of revolutionary committees in all the provinces, the autonomous regions, and the two special municipal areas of Peking and Shanghai.

13–31 October: 12th plenum of the Central Committee, deposing Liu Shao-chi as President of the Republic: actually naming him for the first time in an official communiqué, which also announced that the ninth national congress of the Communist Party would take place in 1969.

21 November: Peking no longer to accept either French francs or pounds sterling in its commercial dealings abroad.

26 November: Peking offers Washington the chance of resuming, on 29 February 1969, the talks between their ambassadors in Warsaw, and suggests that they work out an agreement on the five principles for peaceful coexistence formulated at the Bandung conference.

26 December: Mao is 75.

27 December: Eighth Chinese nuclear explosion.

1969

1 January: *Renmin Ribao*, *Hongqi* and *Jiefangjun Bao* all publish the same editorial, setting out the tasks for the year ahead, in particular that of constituting a completely new-style Communist Party – with new statutes, new machinery, new membership.

18 February: Taking as its pretext the defection of Liao Ho-chu, China's chargé d'affaires in the Hague, which is described as a 'serious anti-Chinese incident', Peking notifies the U.S.A. by an official note from the Ministry of Foreign Affairs of the postponement *sine die* of the 135th ambassadorial meeting in Warsaw to have taken place on 20 February.

2 and 15 March: Violent incidents between Chinese and Russian border guards on Tchenpao–Damansky Island on the Ussuri.

29 March: In a long note amounting to a lesson in history, Russia suggests to China that they resume the negotiations interrupted in 1964 on the frontier problem. The Soviet declaration is described by Peking on 31 March as a 'tissue of lies and calumnies'.

1 April: Opening in Peking of the Ninth Congress of the Chinese Communist Party.

CHINA READINGS

(*Three volumes*)

Edited by Franz Schurmann and Orville Schell

The most comprehensive and authoritative work on
China ever published here in a popular edition. Prepared
and introduced by two leading sinologists, it contains
material on Chinese politics, ideology, society, and
culture from a wide range of original and secondary
sources, both Chinese and foreign. It is intended to
clarify contemporary China's traditions, motives and
attitudes as they have emerged from her history, rather
than offer a merely chronological account.

Volume 3

COMMUNIST CHINA

This volume brings the story from the triumph of
communism in 1949 up to the present day and the
latest, still unresolved, upheavals. Although their
ultimate aim remains the establishment of a communist
society, Chinese leaders have alternated between
visionary and practical approaches to this ideal.
Extravagant attempts at violent change, such as the
Great Leap Forward and the famous Cultural
Revolution, have been interspersed with periods of patient
planning and even an interlude of liberalism (the
Hundred Flowers campaign). This volume, which
includes material by Mao Tse-tung, Lin Piao, Chou
En-lai, Dean Rusk and Edgar Snow, provides much of
the evidence necessary for interpreting Chinese ideology
and policy in the age of the Sino-Soviet split and the
Cultural Revolution.

Not for sale in the U.S.A. or Canada